RESURRECTION

By Nick van der Leek

Copyright (c) 2014 by Nick van der Leek

All rights reserved. No part of this book may be used, reproduced or transmitted in any form or by any means, electronic or mechanical, including photocopying, recording, or by any information storage or retrieval system, without the written permission of the author, except where permitted by law, or in the case of brief quotations embodied in critical articles and reviews.

Cover design: Nick van der Leek

Acknowledgements

This third narrative in a series of five would not be possible without the encouragement, support and commitment of several people. Ray Wicksell, Leonard Carr, Ulrich Roux and David Dadic, thank you for making yourselves available at no cost, and sometimes for considerable lengths of time, to contribute to this narrative.

Thank you to Bertus Preller, another advocate, for your ideas and insights. Also Sheetal Schneider and Maricelle Botha, both journalists who've taken an interest in the narrative beyond the narrative.

Jacques Steenkamp, Alec Hogg, Margaret Taylor, Vernon Baumann and Terry Wittwen for your coaching, reviews, suggestions, endorsements and general enthusiasm.

I've made extensive reference to Dr Ross Tucker, Prof Tim Noakes, and the efforts of numerous other writers, including Kathryn Schulz, Michael Sokolove and Jonathan McEvoy. I hope I haven't quoted you too liberally. Equally, I hope I have not quoted you too insubstantially.

There's a reason a narrative like this needs to exist. A counterfeit narrative exists in the public domain. Consistent effort, leveraged by global media, has put this invalid narrative in place. What counterevidence is there to correct, and contradict, the extraordinary imbalances in these narratives? I will leave it to the *conscientious* reader – who also deserves special mention, and special acknowledgment – to evaluate whether *Resurrection* corrects these imbalances sufficiently, or not.

Table of Contents

Acknowledgements 3
Introduction 6
Oscar has come back from the dead before 10
Heroism, heartache and hype 11
What do you think is the future for Oscar? 13
Wicksell on Pistorius – Paralympian or Olympian, Valid or Invalid? Part 1/2 15
Wicksell on foiled ambitions, and Oscar's journey to success with the Wicksells Part 2/2 28
The Road to Resurrection begins with an Appeal 42
Case Law – Salem Witch Trials, New Zealand's David Baine, OJ Simpson, Griekwastad and Brown v National Director of Public Prosecutions 48
"Just because you do not take an interest in politics doesn't mean politics won't take an interest in you."— Pericles 49
Heroism? 65
Lignano – the sunny home of heartache and heartbreak 74
Parallels with Caster Semenya 80
The Circus Comes to Town 89
What's it *really* like to be Oscar? 93
Blade Runner = Superman? 97
Transcendence 100
Oscar vs Oliveira & Discernment 105
Bullshit 111
A (Feel) Good Story 118
Heartache: 4 Shots in the Dark 133

The Context of Pressure in 2013 136
Heartbreak Hotel: Are you going or staying? 139
Our own narratives stray far from objective truth 147
Last Stop for the PR Train? 151
Is it a Conspiracy? 159
Note to the reader: 162
"Did he involve her in his career?" 164
The Agent's Two Key Revelations 176
Motive – the undiscovered country 208
Conclusion 224
Author's Note: 228
Author's Update [11 November 2014] 230
About the Author 233

Introduction

Returning to Innocence – by Leonard Carr

The process of restoring innocence is similar to the process of redemption and reconciliation in the spiritual sphere. It is the process by which we restore wholeness in our important relationships. The process starts with full disclosure and explicit acknowledgment of our wrongdoing. Healing comes on the heels of the profound regret that overtakes one's entire being. To the extent that we make ourselves responsible, we are also healed and restored. The deeper the admission of responsibility, the deeper the potential healing.

The narrative to follow in this process is as follows:

1. **I regret what has happened** as well as my part in what has transpired. I did not want this to happen to me, to you or to us.

2. **I recognise the consequences** that this event or dynamic has had for me, for you and for us. I recognise it both on the level of intellectual understanding and on an emotional level in that I empathise with your feelings too.

3. **I take full ownership** and responsibility unequivocally and unconditionally for my participation in what transpired without defence, excuse, justification or diversion of responsibility.

4. **I regret deeply** with all my heart any envy, resentment, pride, arrogance, obstinacy, vainglory, insensitivity, complacency, ignorance, lack of empathy and compassion in me that informed partially or completely my behaviour towards you.

5. **I commit to deeply listening** to your needs and feelings until I fully understand them and appreciate what you need to feel, hear and see in order to fully believe that I truly wish to make amends.

6. **I will use that knowledge** to move to a place within myself that will give you the reassurance and confidence that I will to the best of my ability become the person that I need to be for you to feel safe enough to restore the innocence in the relationship.

7. **I commit to let go** of and not re-evoke or add to my own epistle of past hurts and disappointments. I commit to going forward with a new start and to forgiving and forgetting.

Resentment is simply an alibi for not taking responsibility for creating a positive future. Your behaviour cannot be caused by the past because all decisions that you make are made with reference to the future.

The most dangerous belief you can harbour is that you do not have the power, ability or necessary life conditions to make a difference and to create the relationships that you most prefer. Related to this belief is the idea that something or someone else would need to change for you to enjoy the quality of relationships that you most desire.

Another obstacle to real forgiveness is that to admit that you have gone wrong might mean acknowledging that you have been destructive or been doing wrong for a long time and have in the process lost a lot of time, damaged your life or relationships and destroyed potential. Forgiveness often entails forgiving yourself first for your own mistakes that stem from misunderstanding, blindness, laziness, stubbornness, conceit, ignorance, poor judgment, over reactions, hyper-sensitivity and other weaknesses of being human. In essence you need to forgive yourself, others and life itself for not living up to your expectations or ideals or for not turning out the way that you would have preferred.

In essence it is about being able to accept your imperfection and human frailty and having the humility to view and accept yourself as a very ordinary person. This means not judging and not comparing yourself to an infallible angel or a god.

Oscar has come back from the dead before

Amputation > IAAF battle > Boat accident >

Can he do it again?

If Oscar is diagnosed with an anxiety disorder, he will walk. – comment on CBS 48 Hours 'Shots in the Dark' Episode.

And if he walks, will he ever run again?

Heroism, heartache and hype

You are the authority on what is not possible, aren't you...? They've got you looking for any flaw, that after a while that's all you see. For what it's worth, I'm here to tell you that it is possible. It is possible. - Vincent, in Gattaca

This narrative seeks to interrogate Oscar's, the media's and our own interior narrative. It seeks to assess how authentic they are which is an indication of how authentic *we* are, as a society.

Who are our heroes? How honest is our media? How honest are we about ourselves? How useful are heroes and models to our cultural heroism, and what does that say about us? Finally, what is the nature of heroism? These are the questions this narrative will attempt to answer.

The short answer is that *Resurrection* - another word for

>reappearance

>renaissance

>rebirth

>renewal

>revivification

is *always* heroic. But is it possible for Oscar? And can it be possible for us too?

Now let's examine the details. We're going to look carefully at Oscar's own narrative. Who he says he is, what those close to him say and what the experts say. How has the media spun this all together? What's been put in and what's been left out. And then, we'll take those observations and hold them up like a mirror. Because in the end, the value and the meaning of this narrative comes down to not only how we view Oscar Pistorius, but how we view ourselves. Individually and collectively.

What do you think is the future for Oscar?

Jor-El: *He will need that advantage to survive. Their atmosphere will... sustain him.*
[He looks at his son and walks over to the area where the ship that will carry Kal-El lies. There are information crystals placed in slots on the edges]
Lara: *He will defy their gravity.*
Jor-El: *He will look like one of them.*
Lara: *He won't *be* one of them.*
Jor-El: *No. His dense molecular structure will make him strong.*
Lara: *He'll be odd. Different.*
Jor-El: *He'll be fast. Virtually invulnerable.*
Lara: Isolated. *Alone.*
Jor-El: *He will not be alone.*
[He holds up a clear crystal and takes a long look at it]
Jor-El: *He will never be alone.*
[He places it in one of the slots along with the other crystals in the ship]

"To answer that," says Ray Wicksell, Oscar's former agent, "let me just go back for a second. What I wanted him to do for many years, even when he was with Peet [Oscar's agent, and Wicksell's successor], and I haven't spoken to many people about this, only my wife and Oscar, I wanted him to go around the world. Because he's well known now. And I wanted him to go to Mexico, I wanted him to go to Argentina, I wanted him to go to Cuba, I wanted him to go to the United States. Go to Africa. And tell the Oscar Story. How to become a champion in life. You know, not only in work, but in life. And that's what I wanted him to do. And then I wanted him to come out with a book; he came out with his book. But then I wanted him to go into these talks. I mean, he would have been such a wonderful speaker, on stage. Because it comes natural for him. That's what I always wanted him to do."

Then Wicksell pauses. "At one stage," he says, "I told Carte Blanche, 'You know, he will bounce back.' I thought that, if he gets acquitted he might still be able to run the Olympics again. Because, you know, if he's innocent, people forget and forgive very, very quick. If someone is innocent. So I said 'Yes, he'll be back. He's got it in his blood.'"

There's a small addendum to this statement, but we won't go into it here. Not right now. We'll leave it for the end. We have to explore the question first, before we answer it:

Can Oscar come back from this?

How would he?

How could he?

And should he?

To answer these questions we need to spend time understanding how he resurrected himself from an obscure, awkward, pimply faced kid into a GQ cover boy. How did he do that, and how genuine was that hero that the world watched, and yes, loved.

Wicksell on Pistorius – Paralympian or Olympian, Valid or Invalid? Part 1/2

Jonathan Kent: *No, no. Now, you listen to me. When you first came to us, we thought people would come and take you away because, when they found out, you know, the things you could do... and that worried us a lot. But then a man gets older, and he starts thinking differently and things get very clear. And one thing I do know, son, and that is you are here for a *reason*. I don't know whose reason, or whatever the reason is... Maybe it's because... uh... I don't know. But I do know one thing. It's *not* to score touchdowns. Huh? [they laugh]*
Young Clark Kent: *Thanks, Dad.*

Ray Wicksell, a talented US miler, was paid to compete in South Africa by a company with a Zebra as its logo.

Wicksell recalls; "It was a fuel company, called Trek. We had a tour, and some of us stayed, as did Tom Petranoff, the javelin champion, and I. Sometime later Trek brought another American team here. "

Wicksell went on to marry a local Afrikaans athlete , Ilse de Kock, who happens to hold the longest standing record for a female athlete in South Africa.

"What time did she run, and when?"

"2:37 for the 1000m," says Wicksell, "which Ilse set in '82 or '83. Not even Semenya Caster could break it."

Wicksell mentions that Semenya has a new coach, Maria Motala. "But athletes," he says, "don't always make good coaches."

How did you meet Oscar?

"About seven or eight years ago, Oscar asked me if I would represent him, and I said, 'Sure, absolutely.' It started on the track," Wicksell reflects, speaking with a discernible Californian accent. "He was this young kid, with braces. He was still at Boys High [Pretoria Boys High] at the time, young and shy. You know, everything had to pass through his father. His father was his guardian – his mother had passed away. So, he knew of me, and he liked me, and so that's basically how it started."

So the first time Wicksell encounters Oscar is on the track?

"Yeah it was on the track."

Did he need a new coach? Why is he talking to you?

"No, he had a coach already. He needed a good agent. He really needed someone to help him with sponsorships. He didn't have any money. First of all, he didn't even have a shoe sponsorship."

And how old was he then?

"Young, I think he was seventeen or eighteen." Wicksell mentions a guy by the name of MacKenzie. "He's a coloured guy, and a lawyer. You should speak to him. He helped Oscar buy his first house."

How old was he then?

"When he bought his first house? Nineteen years old."

That's quite a growth curve.

So, Oscar as a seventeen year old, asked Wicksell to be his agent. Wicksell said yes.

Then what happened?

"Then I had to get a professional team together. This is something South Africans don't understand; when you pick up a sportsman," Wicksell explains, "you've got to make sure you've got a whole medical team behind him. It doesn't matter which sport is it; cricket, rugby, basketball, soccer… So that's what I did – I still have the actual clipping from the Rapport, with a photograph of the team I put together - eight or nine guys in all. I had a professional chiropractor, two biokineticists, a physiotherapist that massaged him every day, a couple of guys from the University of Pretoria as well as Arnold Geerts from Supersport, myself, and MacKenzie (the lawyer). They're all in the picture. "

What had he achieved at that stage that made you feel justified in putting this 'team' behind him?

"He was one of the best disabled runners. He was winning. And that was important to me. I just thought he had tremendous talent. I could already see – my wife thinks I'm crazy – but I can watch a guy run four of five laps and tell whether they have talent."

Sound farfetched? Actually, Wicksell himself is, or rather was, a world class runner in his day. So was Wicksell's wife, as alluded to earlier, and his daughters are both superlative sprinters. Ray Wicksell has run an incredible 24 sub-four minute miles, and qualified – as an American athlete on the US track team – for the 1980 Olympic Games in Moscow. One of his training partners, before he moved to South Africa and married Ilse, was Steve Scott.

Scott is one of the greatest mile runners in American history. In his career, he ran 136 sub-four minute miles. That's more than any other runner in history. Interestingly, and perhaps even crazier than his legendary sub-mile records, Scott is seen as the founder of 'speed golf'.

He started this 'fad sport' in 1979 and three years later set a world record for the fastest round of golf on a regulation course. The point is, Scott, an incredible athlete by any measurement, was Wicksell's training partner. Scott recognised Wicksell's potential to crack the four minute mile before Wicksell fully believed it himself. The first time Wicksell broke the barrier was in a pair of shoes given to him by Scott who told him, effectively; "Maybe you can do it in my shoes." And of course, he did. The upshot of this fragment of back-story is that great athletes are great at recognising the abilities and potential of other great athletes. We're going to come back to Wicksell in a minute.

Note: The reader may be interested in the writer's personal view, at this point. It is informed to some extent by a quote that the media either seem to miss, or have been filtering out of Oscar's fairy tale. And it comes from Oscar himself. If you, the reader, have been following much of the coverage, chances are you've already seen it. If not, it's time to go here:

http://www.cbsnews.com/videos/oscar-pistorius-shots-in-the-dark/

Shift the slider in the video to exactly 10:30 and allow a moment for buffering as the video loads on your device. The same teenage boy Wicksell met is in the picture. He modestly admits: "God had a plan when he gave me these legs. At the end of the day I'm happy. I don't think I would have been doing athletics if I was able-bodied."

This does not necessarily contradict Wicksell's assertion that Oscar had tremendous potential. But what it does show is Oscar himself had a strange relationship with his 'new' prosthesis. They were effectively making him both into who he was, and who he wasn't. Confused? Well, it *is* a little confusing. It probably confused the hell out of Oscar, and if you got close enough to him, you probably started sensing that inner tension. Because here's the thing: There's no doubt Oscar wanted to have it all. The determination and ambition were there. He wanted to make his mark, and his prosthesis (and especially the latest space-age tech embedded in his artificial limbs) could give him an entirely new lease in life. So why not run with it? Oscar did, and let's be fair, those legs don't run themselves. They needed a fit, healthy, focused, motivated engine to keep them balanced, integrated, operational and fast. And history shows the half man, half carbon fibre hybrid was extremely effective, and extremely compelling. That's why Oscar caught on in the public imagination here and, around the world, like a brushfire in winter.

Let's face it, it had the elements of a heroes quest, on the scale of Odysseus, Prometheus or Icarus. Take your pick, but for a while it really was about this young man undergoing *Resurrection*.

His mother had died. His father wasn't really in the picture. His siblings were able-bodied. Who was he in the world? Who could he be? What if he could be something beyond himself? What if he could transcend his disability, and in that heroic quest, the world would embrace him as their own. The Prodigal Son. Received, acknowledged and accepted by the world.

Perhaps somewhere in there was a message to his mother, and also his father. Was it a deeply held sense of mission? You better believe it. Because for Oscar that's the core of it. "God had a plan when he gave me these legs."

God gave him those legs. God would raise him…like a son…is an inference some might make. And the overall effect? *Resurrection*.

Except beliefs and goals and dreams are not enough. You need to train and do the work. You need a team behind you, supporting you. And that's where Wicksell came in. And somewhere along the line the legs (or leglessness) got left out of the narrative. What we cared about became what Oscar cared about. Winning. Winning at all costs. And if Wicksell could do anything, it was deliver a winner, a young man who wanted to win and win the hearts of the world.

"I can see whether a guy has talent," Wicksell says. "Not to brag, I could be the best sports scout in this country. The first place I would go to, to recruit athletes would be the coloured townships of Cape Town. That's the first place I'd go."

But Oscar is not a conventional athlete. "Yeah, he was running on his blades, and he was winning everything. You know, I just thought at the time, he had tremendous talent. And he could really blossom, at that level. I never ever thought he'd run in the able-bodied [races]. No way I saw that coming."

Was your perception based on sheer speed, perhaps compared to the speeds you ran once?

"Yeah. It was based on his talent, his talent at running like that with a disability, mainly. I wasn't looking at it from the perspective of 'normal athletics', I was looking at from the perspective of his ability as a disabled runner."

It's at this point, because of course we (me the writer, you the reader, and Wicksell, who was there at the time *with* Oscar) – find ourselves intruding into the original narrative. Which was Oscar saying, at the advent of his self styled *Resurrection*:

"I don't think I would have been doing athletics if I was able-bodied."

Isn't the implication obvious? As an able-bodied athlete would he not have been, for all intents and purpose, just an ordinary mortal? Had Pistorius had normal legs, he would be no better than an average college athlete. So the reasoning goes. Even he seems to accept this as a given.

But then the narrative changes. As Oscar achieves worldwide fame (as a Paralympian), and secures sponsorships worth millions, he feels increasingly entitled to race with and against able-bodied runners. It becomes a circus. It becomes court battles, and contentiousness. Does he have an advantage or doesn't he? Should he or should he not compete? The circus changes the game completely, and it's a very high stakes game. The highest. Millions are hanging in the balance.

Can anyone imagine Oscar saying, in court, to the IAAF (who would later change tack and want to *prevent* Oscar from competing with able-bodied runners) – can we imagine Oscar saying to them:

"You know what, I'm going to be honest with you. I don't think I would have been doing athletics if I was able-bodied."

Would he say that to Jay Leno following his triumphs at the London Olympics? He was the Games' brightest star in 2012, his star was at its zenith, bright enough to eclipse the likes of Usain Bolt.

But:

"I don't think I would have been doing athletics if I was able-bodied."

Then why do it if you're not?

Back to Wicksell: "He wanted to make the Olympic team," Wicksell explains. "He wanted to break records. All that. He had strong goals, already at a young age."

Did you say to him, 'You should go for the Olympics?'

"No, he said it to me. I think true champions know it within. I mean, I didn't have to tell him that he could make the Olympic team. I think he already knew he had enough talent to do that."

Of course Wicksell is talking about the Paralympics here. Even in Oscar's most grandiose ambitions, the idea, in those early days, of competing against able-bodied runners – I'm speculating – wasn't *his own* originally, but came via the IAAF circa 2008. (This is treated exhaustively in 'Recidivist Acts'. Read the chapter titled: Able-bodied but mentally disabled?) Interestingly, whenever it comes up, Oscar's explanation is that he 'always' did sports with able-bodied children. But that's not quite true. For a substantial period of Oscar's schooling, at least according to one of his teachers, he didn't do sport, and when he did, he performed poorly.

Of course we know what happened. The blades were introduced, and the game changed. Oscar took wing. He took off. The higher he flew, the more his momentum seemed to increase as well. Oscar seized this opportunity at heroism with gusto, and I think even the IAAF were surprised when they realised they 'may have made a mistake' inviting him to compete with able-bodied runners, how hard Oscar could fight back. Because by then Oscar's brand had caught on worldwide, and they could spoil the party. Were they going to be the 'bad guy'? Were they going to spoil the sport by literally being 'spoilsports' (in the public's perception). No. Anyway, what harm could one exception make? So they backed off – and let him have the run of things.

It was good for sport, good for the spectators, and – by all appearances – good for Oscar. It was a good story, wasn't it?

Except:

"God had a plan when he gave me these legs."

And:

"I don't think I would have been doing athletics if I was able-bodied."

When you deviate from what you originally think, believe and habitually do, this is called 'reframing' one's own narrative. Reframing is sometimes necessary. It can lead to success, but it can also lead to crisis if it's too much at odds with what's really going on.

Was God's plan that he *Resurrect* himself to the heights of the Paralympics? Or did the plan for Oscar's *Resurrection* go beyond even that? Was God's plan that he ingratiates himself amongst able-bodied runners? And call this fair play?

The reader might see this line of interrogation as unfair or even cynical, but consider the impact it had to have on Oscar himself. To compete against the best able-bodied athletes in the world – if you're going to take that on – what does that involve? Remember, I've pertinently pointed out that there has probably been a shift in Oscar's own narrative. It happened when the IAAF offered him the chance to run with able-bodied athletes. It wasn't just a gesture. It was an invitation with *tremendous* symbolic import for Oscar. Because it was effectively an invitation that included the following subtext:

You've achieved parity. You're one of us. We're offering you a chance to be an equal.

Oscar could be validated at the highest possible level. That's what he wanted.

But an invitation is one thing. What about reality? Was he *really* being validated by this new adventure? Let's personalise this question.

If the IAAF invited you and then withdrew the invitation, even if you'd won the right to validate yourself – and then you're earning millions while you're at it, are your actions VALID?

You can stand on that track, have crowds in their thousands cheering your name, millions – billions even – watching on television. But what's actually going on is you have a full complement of world class track stars, and then there's you – on your prosthetics.

"I don't think I would have been doing athletics if I was able-bodied." Who *really* belongs on that track?

There's not only the self doubt, but there's also the nagging voices (the dissenters) in the background. And so every time you compete, every time you perform, you also have to justify why you are. How do you do that when inwardly you know, "I don't think I would have been doing athletics if I was able-bodied."

Why do you deserve to be there? Because of the legs that aren't me, or because of me? Which part is the champion? And off the track, when you're socialising with the best physical specimens in the world, if your narrative is all about the fact that your disability isn't a factor, that's a hell of a lot of pressure to put on yourself. And this is the critical point. It is one thing to be a world champion Paralympian. And it's a great thing. It's another thing to try to be a champion Olympian when both your legs were amputated as an infant. Is it a bridge too far? Is it overreach?

Certainly with Wicksell, the idea was to conquer the former. The Paralympics. And this was Oscar's *true* Resurrection. This was the real deal, and of course, a real feather in Wicksell's cap.

[Note: the term 'feather in your cap' originates from the customs of some aboriginal warriors, notably the American Indian, where a warrior adds a new feather to their head-gear for every enemy slain. Another form of the same ritual is to celebrate the successful shooting or capture of a game bird during hunting.]

Earlier I used the word 'VALID' and it's an easy word to use and forget about. But what does it really mean. Let's examine the word up close.

Valid means:

- Suitable
- Applicable
- Convincing
- Compelling
- Legitimate
- Official
- Well founded
- Legal

The word valid may just be a word, but when you check through those words, think about how it feels to be challenged – constantly – on whether who you are, what you are doing is and how you are doing it, is 'legitimate'. Is it suitable? Is it even convincing? What do you have to do to be convincing?

If these seem like small questions, watch the 1997 film *Gattaca* with Ethan Hawke. In brief it involves two brothers, in a world where perfect children lead one life, and 'invalid' members of society (the multitude of sad, flawed, naturally conceived individuals) lead quite another life. Ethan plays Vincent Freeman. He wants to belong. He wants to go to the stars. And so he 'pretends' to be a 'VALID' member of society. That pretence comes at great cost. To himself, and to everyone he cares about. It is traumatic. There's a desperation built into every action, every ritual, every carefully constructed ruse.

The biggest deception of course is the most obvious – one's own appearance. Trying to appear – physically – Valid. There is an excruciating scene where Vincent's disabled 'sponsor' (whose identity he has taken possession of) must pretend to be able-bodied when investigators visit his house, looking for Vincent. We see Jerome (Jude Law) climbing up a staircase in his house, using his arms, because his legs don't work. He puts in a colossal effort simply to reach a chair, then wipes off the perspiration on his forehead and, remaining seated throughout, wears the veneer of self-righteous, self-entitled arrogance that is the signature of the overly-validated.

The irony is, this is an act. It's all an act.

You realise though, watching this film, behind the acting is a life and death struggle. Those words aren't used by accident here. There's a scene in *Gattaca* where the valid brother races the invalid brother in the sea. It becomes a life and death struggle for both, because the one validates himself through the other. In other words, if one validates oneself entirely through one's performance, entirely through external stimulus, then one's identity is entirely outside of yourself. And then, a race can literally become a race where one's life is on the line.

Winning = validation = life.

Losing = invalidation = death.

Now let's shorten that: invalidation = death

When Vincent (an Invalid) beats his brother Anton (a Valid), his brother, breathless, despairing, nearly drowning, cries out:

Vincent, how are you doing this?

Vincent: You want to know how I did it? This is how I did it, Anton: I never saved anything for the swim back.

Now let's flip the coin, and consider the lot of the 'Invalid'.

Invalid

- Unacceptable
- Unsound
- Untrue
- Unfounded
- Illogical
- Null
- Void
- Worthless

But the above are all adjectives. Consider Invalid as a noun or a verb

1. Noun: a person made weak or disabled by illness or injury.

"she spent the rest of her life as an invalid"

2. Verb: remove (someone) from service because of injury or illness.

"he was badly wounded and invalided out of the infantry"

Do you see why it's so critical to Oscar's story?

Validation is part and parcel of his *Resurrection*. But validate yourself beyond a certain point, and it is no longer convincing. Not to God, and not even to yourself. And that's when Icarus finds himself too close to the sun, and the wax gluing those wings – knitting the prosthesis to the skin – starts to melt. What happens then? The wings separate. And we see Icarus is not a winged creature after all. We see Oscar is not an athlete after all. He's a legless man. He's been a legless man all along.

Wicksell on foiled ambitions, and Oscar's journey to success with the Wicksells Part 2/2

"The world loved him because he was lovable." – Ray Wicksell

Let's agree that the Resurrection narrative spans 3 legs. The first leg is his rise to become Paralympic world champion. The second leg is his rise to race alongside able-bodied runners. The third is: can he rise after what he did on February 14, 2013?

The reader should know that I've purposefully reconstructed the narrative with Wicksell in this way, because I want to plant the *Gattaca* seed (of Valid/Invalidness) firmly in the back of your mind, *before* I guide you the reader further along the first leg of Oscar's *Resurrection*.

Since we've got the authentic narrative sorted out now, Oscar's original (disabled – valid) and subsequent (able-bodied –invalid) narrative, let's look at how Wicksell's adventure with Oscar, (in other words the first leg), unfolded at face value.

Kudos to Wicksell, it's an impressive story. Let's move into it now.

Nike. Wicksell is very tight with Nike.

Did he arrange deals between Nike and Oscar?

"You know what happened is he always wanted to wear Nike, and at the time he was getting some Nike equipment, but I didn't finalise the Nike International deal. That was done later, once he became very, very famous. And that was an easy deal. I think Peet (Oscar's current agent) did that. You know he was the easiest guy in the world to get brands on. He was like a Tiger Woods. You go to Nike, 'Yes, how much?' You go to Oakley, 'Yes, how much.'"

Does Wicksell recognise anything in Oscar, in himself? After all, Wicksell himself made it to the Olympics. Right?

"You know, I didn't make it into the Olympic team in 1980, but Carter boycotted us because of [the 1979 Soviet invasion into] Afghanistan. In '84 I was an alternate. I had to wait for someone to get injured. So I couldn't run in '84 [those Olympics were held in Los Angeles, Wicksell's backyard], because no one got injured. In '88 I went to the finals and I didn't make the team. So to answer your question, no. I made the team but we couldn't compete."

So what were the first brands you connected him with? And in those early days, were they difficult to get?

"It was easy to get him stock. But to get him a contract was harder because he wasn't really at that level yet. He was winning, but he was just coming onto the scene. So I got some Vitamin companies onto him, like Herbalife. And I got him Nike gear. But the first thing I did, before the gear, before the brands, was get the Medical Team together. That was crucial. You know everyone used to call me Jerry Maguire, because that football player in the movie is from Arizona State. And that's my alma mater. At one stage I was one of the top agents in the states, huh! I loved it. And I would love to do it here. Because there's a gap and I look at it differently, Nick. I look for sponsors, but it's also about growing 'em. And I look beyond their contract and also their career. I mean, what are they going to do after they're finished with their career?"

This of course is the pertinent question. This is the purpose of the entire narrative you – the reader – are holding in your hands. What happens to Oscar now? What sort of career can he have now? What had he set up that he can manage off the track? There are a couple of answers to these questions, many of which we'll deal with later. What the reader should know, though, is Oscar – at the end of 2012 – told Larry King that, together with the Scotland's University of Strathclyde, he was developing a 'cheap' $500 prosthetic foot. We'll get into the irony of this later.

"The danger with an athlete," Wicksell cautions, "just as you see in Jerry Maguire, is it's just one injury, one hit, and their career is finished. So how do they invest their money? It's very important."

At this point Wicksell reveals he's also represented [Blue Bulls/Springbok Rugby player], multiple Olympian and world champion swimmer Roland Schoeman, and Jacques Freitag, a world champion high jumper.

Remember when Kuwait offered Schoeman plus minus R30 million to swim under their flag? "That was my deal. Three Russians were offered the same deal. They went, and they haven't looked back. At that time, I wanted him to take it. But I think he had a chat with Ernie Els, and Els convinced him to swim for South Africa. Difference is, Els already had all the money in the world. He should have taken that deal!" Wicksell insists. "The package was incredible. He would have had so much money."

"When I was [Blue Bulls/Springbok Rugby player's] agent," he adds, "there were too many other people who wanted to be involved. With [Blue Bulls/Springbok Rugby player] I didn't want to do the full service thing, but I was trying to help him get a car. An Audi convertible. At Nike we had attorneys doing the attorney work, and doing the contracts. And guys like myself doing the deals. We're the dealmakers. I'm a Jerry Maguire. I'm not a lawyer. I make deals. I make things happen, with a Liberty Life, or a Discovery. I make sure the athlete fulfils his sponsorship commitments. He performs, he makes his appearances. He's consistent. I make sure they get their pound of flesh. That's what I do. In South Africa there are too many guys trying to do something they don't know how to do. There are fathers, mothers, shit man! When you look again, you find out he's got another agent!"

[**Sidenote:** There's some discussion on young Chad le Clos, and his potential to have a massive innings. Wicksell reckons "Chad's gotta go with IMG, the guys who handle Tiger Woods." Wicksell has a lot to say about this, but I won't divulge those details here.]

Interestingly, at the same time Wicksell was representing Freitag, the talented high jumper, so was Peet van Zyl (who would go on to become Oscar's agent). "'What are you doing in South Africa? It's indoor season, you're one of the best high jumpers in the world, what are you doing here?' 'No,' he said, 'I can't get into any meets.' I said, 'OK, let me make one call for you.' So I call John Verster, in

Potchefstroom. I say, 'John, can you call your friend that's a race director in Europe, so we can get Jacques Freitag into this indoor meet, and get him competing?' So while we're sitting there, I got him into the meet."

Didn't your daughters train with Oscar?

"You know they trained at the same track, but Stephanie and Eugenie don't want to talk about Oscar. I've had a lot of newspaper people try to contact them, because you know, my girls spent a lot of time with him, at his house. They were like brothers and sisters. But they don't want to talk about it. Even with their friends. Especially Stephanie. She doesn't feel comfortable with it, because she feels very close to Oscar. Oscar used to hold her [starting] blocks, when she ran the 400. And whenever he did she'd win, and it became like a lucky charm thing. And then she would hold Oscar's blocks also. And this would be at big international meetings. Also local meetings. And then Stephanie would stay at his house and travel with him. He'd come and pick up the Wicksell girls and take them out to dinner. So they don't want to say anything, whether it's positive or negative. They're kind've…shying away from this whole thing."

Wicksell says an agent needs to keep his charge stable, and feels Oscar's agent

"Me as an agent I would have gotten more involved in his romantic life. When you go out with woman you can't stay out late. Girls tend to keep you up. A champion has to live like a clock."

"You know, Oscar had a lot of girlfriends. My kids were like sisters to him, and they had their own boyfriends at the time. And Oscar only had friendships with them. But Peet could have looked after him better, maybe, in that sense."

And on the track? What sort of experience did Wicksell share with Oscar before or after those 'moments of truth'? The actual races.

Wicksell recounts an interesting story, an encounter that happened:

"Before the Olympics, on a perfect sunny Saturday," Wicksell takes a breath, "what happened is he needed to qualify, and he – you know he never qualified for the Olympic Games? You know that?"

Are we talking able-bodied Olympics?

Wicksell says, "Yes."

Didn't he qualify in the relay? He ran a B qualifying time, but not an A.

"He qualified in the relay but he never qualified in the open [individual] event. But he ran the open and there were a lot of athletes that were upset."

How did that happen?

"I think what happened…but you can check…I think a country can allow an athlete to run if they hit the B standard, but not the A. And a lot of [able-bodied] South African athletes were very upset about that. I have to tell you, I thought that was very unprofessional. But going back to Oscar, they were very upset, the athletes. Because there were some athletes, a lot of athletes, that qualified in B standard times, and they didn't go, they stayed home. So, going back to that day…it was a sunny afternoon, just perfect conditions. And he comes to me against the rail where I was standing, because I wanted to have a chat with him. He was worried. He had a lot of trust and faith in me, but he was very worried about his race. He wanted to run well, but he was worried about the competition. I said to him, 'Oscar, this is the perfect day for you. Don't worry about competition. You're in great shape. I've been watching you train on the track, and the reason you're afraid, is you're afraid of success. You're also afraid of failure, but you're more afraid of how well you're gonna run. The guys are gonna make you run fast; that's what it's all about. That's why you train. So you can run fast.'"

When Wicksell says the word 'fast' in his American accent, with that Californian inflection, there's something magnificent in it. Something glorious beckons in the way he says the word. And of course, this man has lived the word himself. To run a sub-four mile translates to average speed of 24.14km/h. Most gym treadmills only go as high as 19km/h.

Wicksell goes on, telling Oscar that his training isn't just 'to go through the motions'. "You train so that you can get to your personal best. So I told Oscar: 'No matter what, it's going to be fast today, and you can make the race fast. What you've gotta do is run the 400 as if it was a 200. Don't worry about dying! 'Cos people worry too much about getting into lactic acid debt. Run it as a 200; it's perfect.' I said: 'There's nobody here [meaning no real rivals]. Go for it. If you die you die, but you'll die to a great time. If you don't die, you just win.'"

It's hard not to chuckle at this.

Wicksell insists: "Those are the two things. If you don't die, you win. If you die, you die to a great time."

That's a great motivational talk because somewhere in there is the sentiment that if you give it your all, you can't lose. So just *do that* – give it your absolute all.

Wicksell explains he sometimes ran his sub-four minute miles (4 laps on the track) as though it was only a 3 lap race. 'What about the last lap?' people would ask me. I'd tell them, 'Yeah, I was dying. I felt so much lactic acid I was tasting blood in my throat, but you have to experiment.' And you know, he [Oscar] did exactly what I said. I broke down that 400, and he ran his personal best. To date, that is his personal best time."

On this last assertion, I have been able to confirm Wicksell's claim, Oscar ran his personal best (at the time at the Tuks track). He ran a 45.61 for the 400m at the Provincial Championships in Pretoria, in March 2011.

Source: http://supportforoscar.com/athletics.html

From my research Oscar's personal best in the 400 metres came three months later, 45.07, set in July 2011 at the *Meeting Internazionale di Atletica Sports Solidarity* in Lignano, Italy. This is also a Paralympic word record in the T43 (double amputation below the knee) classification. The world record in the 400 for able-bodied athletes is 43.18; set 15 years ago by America's Michael Johnson. We will touch on the relevance on Paralympic world records and the decreasing margin of these to records set by able-bodied athletes, in the following chapter.

But before we move on, an interesting question that nevertheless emerges, on this issue of dying, and lactic acid, is this: if an athlete only has half a limb, or a quarter of a limb, surely less total energy is employed by the remaining tissues of the organism. In other words, surely lactic acid is less of a limiting issue for athletes making use of carbon fibre prosthesis, especially those using two artificial legs, as opposed to one.

Wicksell says Oscar's upper body has to do all the work, and he has to try to breathe and not 'tighten up.' Wicksell also points out that leg speed (or cadence) is related to arm speed. We will touch on this in the next chapter too. For now, take note that official race statistics appear to support the assertion that double amputees are better off (well, faster runners certainly) than single leg amputees. The world Paralympic record on 1 artificial leg, officially termed 'single, transtibial amputation' or T44, is 49.87 seconds, about 4 seconds slower than Oscar's world record.

Coming back to Wicksell, did he encounter Oscar recently? I have a vague recollection, perhaps from Carte Blanche's Oscar Trial channel, where Wicksell mentioned they'd bumped into each other in a parking lot? Wicksell answers, "Yes."

What happened? "The thing in the parking lot was quite a strange thing for me. My daughter had just left for the University of Wyoming [in the States]. And you know I hadn't seen him in months. And this guy parked me in, and I'm tryin' to get out. I was screaming at him, and he came out and he said, 'Ray, it's Oscar.' But he had a full beard, and glasses, and a cap on. He parked me in because he wanted to see me. And he gave me a hug. Shame, he was shaking. And it was a sad moment. And I said, 'I'm so disappointed in you. And Stephanie's gone, and she wanted to see you.' And he said, 'Yeah, it's been very tough.' And he's sorry. And he'll communicate with her on Skype. And SMS. But yeah, you could see, he was going through a very tough time. That's the last time I saw him, and then I was on the front page of the Pretoria News. And they asked me about him, my personal opinion about him as a human being and I just said exactly…I just told the truth. I said, I told the paper, 'I'm not trying to promote Oscar, you know, make him out to be a hero, I'm telling you the true story how he was with me.' And you must remember, it was 17, 18 and 19. I mean, he was a minor. He was just a young kid. They asked me, 'Did you see his anger?' I said, 'No, why would I see his anger?' I was his agent. He loved me. There was no anger. I never saw anger at all, and if I did see anger first of all, I wouldn't have had my daughter spend the night at his house, or allow her to be so close to someone, you know, that's an angry beaver. So we never saw that. My family never saw that.'"

In 2012 a British newspaper, the Guardian, specifically published an article about Fourie and Oscar rooming together.

The Guardian article, penned by Andy Bull, titled *Oscar Pistorius and Arnu Fourie seek room at the top at Paralympics*, was published on September 1, 2012, the first day of the Southern Hemisphere Spring. And based on both Oscar's account and Bull's tongue 'n cheek commentary, everything couldn't have been rosier. It was just quips and world records; two bro's living it up in those unknowable Olympic heights. Here's a direct quote:

Oscar Pistorius had said that he was worried about what the mood would be like in his room in the athletes' village on Saturday night. He is sharing with his South African team-mate Arnu Fourie, and both men are competing in the T44 200m final on Sunday. They are actually grouped in different classes – Pistorius is T43, Fourie T44 – even though both are competing in the same event.

"It is going to be a bit awkward the night before the final," Pistorius said. *"I might have to drop some sleeping pills in his water."*

It turns out that Pistorius will not have to worry too much. They should both sleep well, seeing as they both set world records in the heats. Pistorius beat his own T43 world record of 21.58sec, set in

2007, when he finished the third heat in 20.30sec. In the preceding race, Fourie set a T44 world record of 22.57sec, knocking five hundredths of a second off the time set by the USA's Jim Bob Bizzell in 2008.

If Wicksell and his family never saw anger, who did? Well there is someone. Arnu Fourie. Did Arnu tell anyone about it at the time? Yes, he did. You may have seen the quote before, but in this context it's worth repeating. It's also worth noting that this article wasn't written during the Olympics in July, August, September or at *any* stage in 2012. It was published for the first time a few days *after* Reeva's death.

In other words, no one breathed a word about it. Not even a journalist who knew about it. On February 17, 4 days after Reeva's death, radio journalist David 'O Sullivan (another presenter on the Oscar Trial Channel) published Oscar *Pistorius: Not the boy I knew* in Britain's The Telegraph newspaper. Here's a snippet.

At the London Games, I was chatting to Oscar's roommate in the Athletes' Village, Arnu Fourie, who had just won the bronze medal in the 100m, edging his good friend Oscar out of the medals. Oscar was genuinely elated at his mate's success. They were obviously very close and I asked Fourie what it was like rooming with Oscar. He told me he had been forced to move out, because Oscar was constantly screaming in anger at people on the phone. I thought Fourie was joking and waited for him to smile. But he was serious. I was taken aback. I had never thought of Oscar behaving like that.

I realised he was more complex than I had thought.

But why had Sullivan (and Fourie for that matter) said nothing at the time? Had Fourie complained to ASA? Unlikely, ASA and even Sascoc (up to the highest levels) were solidly behind Oscar. When he lost his temper against Oliveira Sascoc provided the following response (published in South Africa's The New Age newspaper):

As the IPC confirmed they will meet with Pistorius in due course. Sascoc chief executive Tubby Reddy yesterday said his organisation would also raise the matter [Oliveira's blade length] with the Paralympic body.

"Obviously to me this is a new issue, because Oscar has been dealing with it directly with the IPC. As Sascoc, our position is that we will engage in this regard with the IPC officially, but that will be done through the proper channels," Reddy said. Reddy applauded Pistorius for issuing an apology, in which he said his intention was not to detract from the Brazilians' moment of triumph.

"Firstly, the athlete was emotionally upset after the race when he made those remarks. However, I understand that the athlete has issued an apology, and went on to congratulate the winner. I am personally quite happy that he took the step he did," Reddy said.

We see Sascoc not only defending and rationalising Oscar's side, but applauding him in the midst of it. And they go a step further. His organisation would also raise the matter with the Paralympic body. This is despite the fact that Oscar's assertion proved to be unfounded. In other words, though he publicly claimed Oliveira had violated official race rules, in fact he hadn't.

We will delve deeper into the details later, but for now, consider the motive. The difference between Oscar and Oliveira is that Oscar has elected, of his own accord, to keep his blades a specific length. The rules of the Paralympics allow a certain leeway in selecting the appropriate length (within specified mathematic algorithms). But why would Oscar elect to *voluntarily* stick to one length, if the rules clearly permitted different lengths (a specification which meant Oliveira was entirely within his rights to use longer blades, as long as they remained within ultimate limits – which they did).

Well, the answer is simple. Since Oscar was also competing in able-bodied races, he *had* to meet strict biometric criteria, or else face red tape and the sort of scrutiny commensurate to doping violations. In other words, if he wanted to compete with able-bodied athletes, his height couldn't fluctuate.

Oscar was applying the same rules and reasoning applied to able-bodied runners, to other Paralympic competitors; he wanted to impose an 'inflexible' height' limitation on other Paralympic athletes. The reason why this would be patently unfair is simply that each disabled athlete is different. Their injuries differ. Their prosthesis differ. Prosthesis are different to shoes. And Oliveira was a typical example of a young athlete (he was only 20, 6 years Oscar's junior) who was still trying to find both his feet and legs.

In summary, two points ought to emerge here.

    1.   Oscar was angry in private, but did not keep his feelings a secret from his roommate. Such was his anger, his roommate had to evacuate. This suggests a pattern (rather than a single incident) of screaming on the one hand, and also that it was of an intensity sufficient to be disturbing and disruptive. Also, he was screaming into a phone, which means it had to be directed at someone. We know that while Oscar was in London, his girlfriend Samantha Taylor was involved in a dalliance with an older man, who, Oscar has testified, flew to Dubai.

    2.   The second point is that Oscar lost his temper at the same time in public. And on camera.

It is going to be a bit awkward

I was taken aback

Why had Sullivan (and Fourie for that matter) not said nothing at the time? As a photojournalist I can tell you why. Pistorius was a gold mine for stories. Which meant you didn't dare breathe a negative word about him. Not only would Oscar likely scribble your name in his little black book of *verboten* journos, and ignore you henceforth, your employer would more than likely fire you for torpedoing that publications gold digging prospects into perpetuity. Is that good journalism?

It is going to be a bit awkward.

Indeed, it was. Notice, whether the incident had occurred or not, Oscar makes a joke about it to Bull, effectively disassociating himself from discussing what it's *actually* like rooming together. We'll also touch on this tactic, levity-as-pseudo-answer, and other occasions where Oscar has done the same thing. Is it covering up? Is it lying? Is it just charm?

Now, let's get serious about this anger thing. Do we take it seriously, or do we shrug it off? If Oscar has any chance at personal *Resurrection*, we need to know whether he is a hothead or not. Can he be trusted? So here's the real tester. I provide Wicksell with the context that he is a Dad. I have personally met both his lovely daughters, Stephanie and Eugenie. I've done a shoot with Stephanie Wicksell on the track, and published some of those photos in a sports magazine.

I point out that we know what happened. So wouldn't Wicksell and his wife have any concerns if his daughters went to visit Oscar now? Would they be concerned if their daughter's spent the night now?

"Of course. ABC asked me the same question. They asked me, 'Ray, did you know he had guns?' I said, 'No, not at all.' They said, 'Would you allow it, as his agent?' I said, 'Absolutely no.' I said, 'Why would I have a world class athlete have guns?' They said, 'It's a hobby, people do shoot, aren't you aware of that?' I said, 'When do you have time to shoot when you're training for the Olympic Games? I never had time to do anything.' So that – the guns – was a huge surprise."

Wicksell then makes an interesting comment. He comes back to the idea of the 'father figure' and says that is exactly what an agent needs to be to his athlete, and in many respects. "An agent has to guide you. Like a guided missile. But the agent [Wicksell's successor] should have done more. He really should have taken those guns away. He should have looked at the circle of friends this guy hung around with. He hung around with…the Americans call them 'shady characters'. I mean, guys that are bouncers. Guys that are in bars. Guys with guns."

Was this to validate himself not just as a man, but a man's man? A real tough guy? "Well, he loved the celebrity and he loved hanging around with…you know…Francois Hougaard. And the rugby players liked hanging around with him, because wherever they go, coffee shops, there's always press and media and girls around. Some people want to be around fame all the time. But I looked at him as growing him, and developing him. And NBC asked me, 'How did it [Wicksell's business relationship] end, with Oscar?' It ended because I wasn't interested in representing sportsmen. It just takes up too much time. It takes up too much energy. And the return isn't great enough for me."

But Oscar went on to become one of the biggest earners in sport.

Wasn't he sorry he didn't stick with Oscar?

"You know at the end, that was the case. My wife said to me, 'Geez, you should have stuck with him.' But you never know where the future's gonna go. And it's not always about the money. It's also about the time and energy. If I had been his agent I'd be flying all around the world, and what time would I have with my wife and kids? So, you've gotta make your sacrifices. But, you know, I had my fair time with him."

Then Wicksell makes a surprising admission. "He was here a week before the shooting. Yeah. He was having drinks with the Wicksells."

Was it just him? Was Reeva with him? "No, he brought a 400 metre runner over, a guy called Rooney, from Britain. He brought this guy he knew from London to meet Steph. He's a tall guy. I thought he [Rooney] was a high jumper. Apparently, he [Rooney] made the finals at the London Olympics. So he came with Oscar, and he [Oscar] was telling us about this new car, a McLaren Boss, he wants to buy. He was in good spirits."

What did Oscar and Rooney have in common? Rooney wasn't disabled.

"Oscar makes friends with everyone. And then Oscar says, 'Come to South Africa. Train with me. Stay with me.' And that's what he did. You know. Everybody liked Oscar. You know, after I was on Carte Blanche [the Oscar Trial channel interviewed him] a lot of people were shocked at the positive stuff I said about him. But you know what I said backstage? I said, 'The whole world loved him. A year and a half ago everybody loved the guy. And if he had so much hate and anger, why would so many people love him?"

The Road to Resurrection begins with an Appeal

"If we could sniff or swallow something that would, for five or six hours each day, abolish our solitude as individuals, atone us with our fellows in a glowing exaltation of affection and make life in all its aspects seem not only worth living, but divinely beautiful and significant, and if this heavenly, world-transfiguring drug were of such a kind that we could wake up next morning with a clear head and an undamaged constitution—then, it seems to me, all our problems (and not merely the one small problem of discovering a novel pleasure) would be wholly solved and earth would become paradise." – Aldous Huxley

What is an appeal? It's a demand a petition a request. An application – in law – for a case to be reheard.

> 1. *Is Oscar likely to appeal and if so on what basis? And on what basis is he most likely to be granted an appeal?*

Ulrich Roux*: An application for leave to appeal can be made on any grounds where the defence alleges that the Judge made an error in law when applying the law to the facts of a specific case after evidence has been placed before the court by both the State and the defence.

In the event that Oscar Pistorius is convicted I am certain that he will appeal. Many talks have been doing the rounds that the fact that the trial has been televised has rendered it to be an unfair trial. This is of course debatable but certainly a grounds for appeal.

In practice a grounds of appeal would be that the Judge erred in applying the law for instance that she applied the test for *dolus eventualis* incorrectly in that Oscar could not have foreseen that Reeva would be killed when he fired four shots into the bathroom door. This is of course only an example. In my opinion there are no concrete grounds for appeal at this stage but one will of course only be able to accurately comment on this once the Judge has made her ruling.

David Dadic**: I agree entirely with Ulrich. I believe he will most certainly bring an application for leave to appeal which I believe he will be granted. Usually an appellant will rely on numerous grounds of such application an appellant does not usually go with a single issue but will rather allege numerous issues or misgivings in the trial and the judgment to support its application in the hope that at least one (or more) will strike a positive chord with a the appeal judges.

2. How likely is an appeal? Masipa and Nel seem to be closing off all possible doors in order to hold off an appeal. Under what circumstances are appeals generally denied? And in an instance where one has unlimited funds and expert advice what angle/or grounds are most likely to succeed?

Ulrich Roux: An application for leave to appeal will not succeed if the Judge finds that no other court will come to a different ruling when applying the law to the evidence presented before court. Should Oscar Pistorius be convicted I would expect Judge Masipa to grant leave to appeal as she will cover herself. This is a common occurrence in practice.

Judges and Magistrates allow the accused to bring an appeal when they are confident about their ruling as a higher court will of course confirm their finding should they have acquitted themselves well of their task in applying the law to the evidence placed before court.

The Judge has been good thus far. There will be no grounds to take her on review as she has not interfered in the proceedings at all thus far. Nel did well in having Oscar assessed as this would definitely have been a ground for appeal should the application not have been made.

As stated above an application for leave to appeal will only succeed should the judge find that a higher court will come to a different conclusion in applying the law to the facts and evidence placed before court.

The written application for leave to appeal should of course set out where the defence believes the Judge erred in her findings. Upon the Judge applying these allegations to the facts and the law and finds that a different outcome can be reached by a different court she has no option but to grant the leave to appeal.

David Dadic: Again there isn't a single angle as it were. The defence team will allege numerous reasons for their application relating to both fact and law. It's very unlikely that the application will be refused because inasmuch as Masipa will feel confident in her handling of the matter and her judgment she will also know that the appeal process is a natural step in trial process and a full bench of 3/5 judges could find differently to her.

Appeals and reversal of trial courts judgments happen all the time. In fact the irony exists that the more confident a trial judge is with their decision the more confident they are in referring a matter to appeal. It's usually the weak judges who in an attempt to avoid some kind of embarrassment will refuse it. Not the case here Masipa has been brilliant.

Moreover as far having unlimited resources is concerned that obviously helps because the appeal process can be very expensive (to the common man) but I would suggest nothing out of synch with what has already been spent by Oscar on this trail to date.

With respect to Renier's sentiment I am not sure about it being the most expensive trial ever as far as Oscar's legal fees are concerned as there have been many longer high court trials than this one (particularly in the Civil trial world which don't make the papers) but I would assume the costs of the channel and media exposure together with the fees is an entirely different number.

> 3. Take us through the appeals process. It will take place in Bloem. How long is likely to last? Who will be present? What is likely to happen? Can his sentence theoretically be made worse?

Ulrich Roux: Upon the accused being convicted the defence first have to apply for leave to appeal. Should the court refuse leave to appeal they will have to launch a petition to the Supreme Court of Appeal in Bloemfontein after which if granted they will have to have the entire record typed up (remember how much evidence has been placed on record thus far in this matter. One will expect the typed up record to be anything between 50 000 and 60 000 pages.) And provide same to the SCA after which they will have to wait for a date on which the appeal can be heard. This is of course dependent upon the availability of the court.

Once a date has been allocated a date will be given to the parties on which they have to submit their heads of argument which is a summary of the grounds of appeal and where the *court a quo* erred as well as a complete list of the case law relied upon in arguing that the SCA should come to a different finding. The bench can comprise either three or five judges. The Court decides cases upon the record of the proceedings before the lower court and after considering the written and oral arguments presented. Witnesses do not appear before the court and the parties need not be present during the hearing of an appeal.

[Note by the author: This means in the likelihood of an appeal we won't see Oscar. He won't presumably even be called to testify. So an appeal is a totally different scenario to what we're seeing now in the North Gauteng High Court].

Ulrich Roux: A written judgment is usually handed down shortly after the argument. The SCA hears appeals on fact and since there are no jury trials it has a relatively wide discretion to make its own factual findings. Because of this jurisdiction judges have to read the record of the full proceedings in the lower courts.

Should he appeal against sentence only his sentence can be made worse yes. Should he only appeal against the conviction the judges cannot make a different finding on sentence in the event that the appeal against conviction is set aside.

Difficult to say how long it will take. A date for appeal to the SCA should be provided within 18 months after conviction. The physical arguing of the appeal before the SCA seldom takes longer than a day or two. The accused will have a representative arguing before the court whilst the State will also have a representative. In a case such as this it will in all likelihood be the same counsel Nel v Roux.

David Dadic: I can't add much more to this it's very well put and complete answer.

    4.   *If Oscar was your client what would you advise him?*

Ulrich Roux: Difficult to say at this stage as there is no conviction as yet. Should there be a prison sentence imposed as is likely in the event of a guilty verdict I will advise him to take his chances on appeal.

David Dadic: I agree I believe an appeal must be applied for as it is common that trial judgments and sentences are overturned/ reduced at the appeals courts. Moreover his bail will be extended to the hearing of the appeal so assuming he is sentenced to prison he will at least buy himself a bit more time at home pending the outcome of the appeal.

*Ulrich Roux is a director at BDK attorneys. He is an attorney based in Johannesurg and an Ironman triathlete. Follow Ulrich @ulrichroux

David Dadic is a litigation attorney with 17 years experience. He is based in Rosebank Johannesburg and posts his own analysis on Who's your Dadic? a Wordpress blog http://whosyourdadic.com/ **Follow David @DavidDadic

Case Law – Salem Witch Trials, New Zealand's David Baine, OJ Simpson, Griekwastad and Brown v National Director of Public Prosecutions

Perry White: *Lois, Clark Kent may seem like just a mild-mannered reporter, but listen, not only does he know how to treat his editor-in-chief with the proper respect, not only does he have a snappy, punchy prose style, but he is, in my forty years in this business, the fastest typist I've ever seen.*

Not even a basic knowledge of the law is required for this section; however three concepts ought to be understood at the outset, to appreciate the relevance and importance of case law.

If the reader is completely unfamiliar with legal principles such as precedent, *stare decisis* and case law please scroll down to the end of this section for a brief recap.

In sum, it is sufficient to note that case law and legal precedents can guide those involved in legal scenarios, whether judges, lawyers, accused parties, defendants or even the media.

We refer to case law to get a sense of a predictable outcome. One outcome some have begun to speculate on is that this trial may introduce groundbreaking new case law (in other words, precedents).

The new case law the Oscar Pistorius trial will set up, is likely to interrogate the question of: what is the reasonable disabled man?

For the purposes of this narrative, lets go to case law way back in the past, and work our way back.

The first case we will look at is not necessarily relevant from a case law perspective, but we'll look at it as an extreme case where justice was neither seen to be done, nor by all accounts, rational. Why should society care about the legal process? The Salem Witch Trials provide chilling reasons.

Salem Witch Trials

There is a joke floating around Facebook at the moment. Superimposed over a black and white image of a Nazi officer inspecting Holocaust prisoners in a Nazi concentration camp are the words:

"Just because you do not take an interest in politics doesn't mean politics won't take an interest in you." — Pericles

Replace the word 'politics' with 'law' and you end up with roughly the same result. There are people who refuse to pay attention to the Oscar Pistorius trial, and stubbornly refuse to pay attention to the Griekwastad case. They may have their reasons. However, there are many more good reasons why we should all pay attention to the legal processes going on in our courtrooms.

What some South Africans have already noted, with horror and dismay, is the ease with each even the worst offenders are granted bail. In some instances, those out on bail commit further offences. Given the appalling levels of crime in South Africa, stricter bail conditions are certainly one option.

Sometimes, though, laws are too strict, and other times, too open to interpretation, manipulation or misinterpretation. Loopholes exist and clever lawyers know how to use them. Now, let's go back in time to 1692. We're in Colonial America and a fellow by the name of Stoughton, William Stoughton is presiding over a particular case in Salem, Massachusetts.

For interest sake, Massachusetts is situated in the far North of North America, basically in line with the Great Lakes, but further East. Boston is its largest city, and Connecticut, Rhode Island, and New York shoulder its southern boundaries. To the north is Vermont and New Hampshire, and then the Canadian wilderness. The Atlantic lies further East.

Now that we're done with the Geography, let's snap back to the History. Judge Stoughton, a nenerated lawmaker, faced a pretty unusual procedural question:

Should visitations by evil spirits (demons and the like) be admitted as evidence in a court of law? Stoughton decided such evidence was permissable. Too bad for the 150 odd folks who were fated to be sucked into this murky scenario. Nineteen were hanged and the rest imprisoned.

Kathryn Schultz, the excellent author of the aptly titled Being Wrong writes:

If you had been alive at the time, and dreamed one night that the ill-fated Goody proctor was in your bedroom attempting to throttle you, you could have presented your dream as evidence before the court – "as though there was no real difference between G. Proctor and the shape of G. Proctor," in the disapproving words of a contemporary observer.

Strictly speaking this case has no relevance to the Oscar Pistorius murder trial, however, what's certainly worth noting is this idea of a 'unseen intruder' justifying – at the time – some pretty heinous punishments on, let's face it, innocent people.

Schultz adds:

It is a testament to how far the legal profession has come that few things seem more antithetical to the spirit of justice today than the admission of so-called spectral evidence.

Schulz goes on to enumerate some of the valuable lessons legal systems around the world learnt from the travesties of this trial. What counts as evidence? What is admissable? How much weight should be given to certain kinds of evidence?

Now is an opportune time to highlight one line of evidence that wasn't brought up in either this trial or the Griekwastad case. Any guesses what this might be? What is implied in both versions? Both accused have relied on the so-called *swart gevaar*, a term coined by the Daily Maverick's Margie Orford.

Have a look:

http://www.dailymaverick.co.za/article/2014-03-03-heart-of-oscars-defence-imagined-threat-of-a-black-stranger/

Orford nails the question here in her blurb. Did Reeva Steenkamp die because of Oscar's rage, or because of his fear?

When we take that question and look at the Salem Witch Trials, it's an interesting way to test it. But the truth, in this writer's view, may lie somewhere in-between, in an 'and' rather than in an 'either or'.

Schulz again:

What is true within the law is also true far beyond it...evidence is immensely central to our lives. We rely on it in science to expand our technological capacity and advance our understanding of the world. We rely on it in journalism to keep us accurately informed and to hold individuals and institutions accountable to their actions. We rely on it in politics to determine which laws to pass, which policies to implement, and which wars to fight. And we rely on it in medicine to sustain our health…

[Note: If the reader has enjoyed these brief interludes with Schulz, look out for Book #4 in this series, *Restitutions*. The title is derived from the legal principle *restitutio ad integrum*. It's Latin. It means restoration to original condition. We'll examine that in Restitutions and also look at the whole idea of error. What is it. Are there lessons we can learn. What were the biggest mistakes made on Oscar and Reeva's journey and how can we restore things…fix things so they were better than they were. How should the IAAF treat disabled athletes in the future? I'll be interviewing Dr Ross Tucker for his insights, and perhaps by then Oliveira will have set new world records in 2014 (as he did last year this time).]

But let's answer the question, at least from the accused version. According to Oscar and the Griekwastad boy a perceived intruder committed the crimes (or caused the alleged crime to be committed). So why not raise this in court. Why not explicitly raise this issue of terrified white people going to bed, and fearing attack from black criminals. If this is their defense, why not be explicit about it? Simple. In both cases the judges are black.

Before we move on to the next case study, one final word from Schulz (boy, she's good). She quotes Descartes, where he defines error as:

Not believing something that isn't true, but as believing something based on insufficient evidence.

In Oscar's narrative, beyond the trial, regarding his appeal to run with able-bodied runners this is precisely why it happened. Someone, somewhere decided there was insufficient evidence, but went with it anyway. Multiply this by a few million and you have your Man as Myth. *Restitutions* will demonstrate how entire lives are shipwrecked on such simple but also fundamentally simple errors.

New Zealand's David Baine

If the Oscar Pistorius trial is shocking (and it is), and the Griekwastad case is South Africa's 'In Cold Blood' (which is my moniker), then David Baine belongs to a separate section of absolute monstrosity. In the Oscar Pistorius trial one young woman was shot to death, behind a locked door. In Griekwastad the tally is three, and all are family members of the accused, and there is evidence of additional rape and beating of skulls with the butt of his weapons. As horrifying as these are, the David Baine cases is far worse. It's Griekwastad on steroids. Death tally? 5 family members. Both parents, two sisters and a younger brother.

I have studied the merits of this case for some time, but the bottom-lines are the following:

    1. Just as in the Oscar Pistorius and Griekwastad cases, there was only one surviving witness (the accused)

    2. There was 'an orgy of evidence' as someone says in Minority Report, all of which was circumstantial

    3. The circumstantial evidence was compelling

    4. Just as the boy relied on his father as possible scapegoat (saying his father may have raped his sister) Bain suggested his father massacred the whole family before committing suicide.

    5. In all three cases the accused references a letter or words by a loved one, close to death, declaring their love for their alleged murderers.

So what happened to David Bain? He was found guilty. New Zealand was sharply divided on his guilt or innocence, and a media circus erupted as a result. Here's where it gets both interesting and perhaps worrying. After 13 years in jail, Bain was acquitted. He has since been looking for ways to be paid compensation for his 'wrongful imprisonment'.

Interestingly, the position of the New Zealand court is that while he may be found not guilty due to reasonable doubt, the presumption is not strong enough to justify compensation. In order for compensation to be paid, if I understand the case correctly, Bain would have to be retried, and prove his case. The reason he does not, it is suggested, is he is very unlikely to succeed.

Moral of the story – if the reader takes time to study Bain's case history, and you can follow my initial analysis here:

http://english.ohmynews.com/articleview/article_view.asp?menu=c10400&no=385217&rel_no=1

And a much deeper examination here:

http://www.nickvanderleek.com/2012/08/david-bain-closer-look-at-someone.html

What the Bain case shows is how easily an accused can literally get away with murder. Even when there is an orgy of evidence. How? The law actually requires a very heavy burden of proof, to protect the innocent. As such, the law would rather allow hundreds or thousands to escape prosecution, if only to guarantee that an innocent accused is not wrongfully convicted. This may be a feather in the cap of a legal system (as a closed system), but ultimately, the failure to convict means criminals are then free to rape, murder and pillage again, and invariably they do. These are the *Recidivist Acts* that are an affront to society. To eviscerate these criminality, attritions eroding at the façade of society, we have to shine massive lights on organisations and individuals. We have to pay attention and care enough to take action. Evil prospers when good men do nothing, and good men are wont to do nothing.

This is one reason behind the particular series of books I have written. If only one could wake society up to who and what underlies our political, economic and social malaise. If only we could recognise the real sporting and moral champions from the frauds and pretenders. The courts may come out with a clean conscience, but society pays the price for this, and when we are distracted (as all of us are these days), these costs can be great.

This is why the Oscar Pistorius trial is of such immense value not only to South Africa and our legal system, but to many others nations, and theirs. We need to be aware of these processes, and overhaul them, modernise them where necessary. Technology, whether twitter, cameras or audio streams, can continue to make major inroads in making these systems and processes accountable to the people they are meant to protect and serve.

Remember, the reason murderers and rapists are punished is not merely a question of holding them accountable, but supremely, for our protection. Who best can speak for societies interests than ourselves, and how better, through the massive real time interactive power of social media.

Hence, as mentioned earlier in this section, the public and society need to pay attention to the standards applied in law. These standards are intended as representative and reasonable standards. Many members of the public may be horrified at how unreasonable some of these standards actually are.

For reference, if Judge Masipa were to acquit Oscar on his version, one can imagine a slew of criminals using exactly the same defence overnight. I killed X (behind a door, curtains etc) because I thought X was an intruder. By the same token, if Judge Masipa accepts the anxiety disorder defense at face value (I was nervous so I shot X by accident) South African courts can expect a deluge of similar defences.

Before we conclude on the Bain case, have a look at this snippet of relatively recent (January 13, 2014) news on what Bain's been up to after his acquittal:

David Bain's right-hand man at his wedding was a convicted murderer, rapist and former prison cell mate.

Paul Russell Wilson, who served 15 years for raping and murdering his 21-year-old girlfriend in 1994, stood beside Mr Bain at the altar during his Christchurch wedding on Friday, as he tied the knot with partner Liz Davies.

The killer was part of a three-man bridal party, which also included long-term Bain champion Joe Karam's sons Matthew and Richard.

More info here:
http://www.nzherald.co.nz/nz/news/article.cfm?c_id=1&objectid=11185381

What we see with David Bain is the supreme precedent for Oscar Pistorius, and the Griekwastadboy for that matter. What it shows is that at any point, a conviction can potentially be overturned, and an accused than return to the world, effectively, none the worse for wear. In David Bain's case – let me be frank – I am appalled both by the ignorance of the New Zealand public and by Bain's virtual celebrity status. There is something similar in the Griekwastad case, where the boy was also said to revel in his newfound 'bad boy' popularity. How this is even possible, where someone is accused of violently destroying the bodies and lives of not one but several intimate family members, that the public still find a way to admire and support such individuals, I struggle to understand.

We have seen the same thing with Oscar too, via the Pistorians. All these people base their beliefs on 'insufficient evidence', and what's more, triumphantly claim that either the evidence doesn't matter, or that no matter what the outcome, their beliefs are unshakeable. These folks do a disservice to the fabric of society, not least to the principles of justice that have been put in place to protect them and us.

OJ Simpson

Much has been said about the similarities of the Oscar Pistorius trial and the OJ Simpson case. There are only a few points to add to these debates.

1. OJ Simpson is serving jail today not for the crime of murder (he was acquitted) but for another, less crime. In other words, his recidivism caught up with him. If Simpson did not murder Simpson and Brown, the person who did has never been found, and no one is looking for him.

2. The OJ Simpson trial, like David Bain, hinged on reasonable doubt. Its likely Oscar's case will too, with the difference being, Oscar has been his own worst enemy when giving his own testimony. Simpson didn't testify in his own defences.

3. Have a look at this link

http://www.nickvanderleek.com/2014/06/oj-and-oscar-trials-combination-of.html

to see where Simpson incriminates himself.

Griekwastad

The importance of the Griekwastad case, briefly:

1. The boy, despite circumstantial evidence, was found guilty on all charges.

2.   Despite mountains of evidence, the local community has appeared to be broadly supportive of the boy

3.   Being a minor, the boy automatically qualifies for a appeal

4.   The maximum sentence for a minor is 25 years. Had the boy commited the offences 3 months later, he would – as a sixteen year old – have been old enough to be sentenced to life in prison.

5.   A passage or three from Jacques Styeenkamp's bestselling The Griekwastad Murders are worthy of closer scrutiny:

What concerned me was that those who believed him to be innocent didn't form their opinion based on a lack of evidence; they were influenced by the fact that he was so young. They simply could not comprehend how a child could pick up a gun and execute three people like animals. People who think like that scare me.

And me.

...Marina Steenkamp...had moved to the back right-hand corner of the courtroom...Every time Cloete asked the boy a question, he would look at her and she would indicate yes or no with a shake of her head...

And then there's this:

> *But the most horrific image I saw that day – and it is a part of this case that will haunt me for the rest of my days – was a close-up of Marthella's disfigured face. Gone was the beautiful girl portrayed in almost every picture I had seen of her. Two purple eyelids held back two oversized eyeballs, which, from appearances, had been forced out of their sockets by the impact of the blows she had suffered to her head. Her face was covered in blood; even her nose and mouth seemed contorted. She had died violently and must have endured excruciating pain prior to breathing her last. I looked at these photos on the screen, and then I looked at the accused, who still appeared completely unaffected by the sight. It made me very, very angry.*

It is time to state the obvious. Even in the context of this trial, the narrative is 99% about Oscar. There is no visceral realisation of what the young, skinny Reeva endured when one bullet after another ripped through her body. Why Gerrie Nel has not had an actual model pose to show positions and injuries is a mystery. Why he has not provided a schematic for Oscar to plot his exact movements, is also strange.

One thing is certain. In all this, Reeva is the real victim. Reeva has been deprived of her life, and she also suffered terribly in her final moments of life. To be killed by a third bullet means experiencing at least two bullet wounds first. One was said to rip through her hip, causing so much damage she couldn't stand. The second ripped through her arm, causing what one expert witness described as 'similar to an amputation'.

The reader needs to activate the imagination and image a scene vivid with screaming, deafening gunshots, multiple gunshots, and blood.

While the boy has not been sentenced yet, what we can say is the judge in the Griekwastad case appears to appreciate the gravity and severity of the crime, circumstantial evidence notwithstanding. Given that Oscar's judge is a woman, and a former social worker, she is likely to do the same.

Brown v National Director of Public Prosecutions

The reader can follow the link below to study the details of this case in its entirety.

http://www.saflii.org/za/cases/ZAWCHC/2011/386.html

The main aspect to highlight here, which has relevance to the Oscar Pistorius trial, is the possibility that the media be used as a scapegoat in the defence's application for an appeal.

This possibility has already been alluded to earlier in this narrative.

The defence may well claim that due to the television coverage of the trial, Oscar right's to a fair trial were impinged in some way. Witnesses may have been anxious or reluctant to testify. Oscar's own anxiety disorder may have been exacerbated by the *in situ* media glare.

But while this may seem a possible grounds for appeal, it may not necessarily be granted, as the Brown case demonstrates. In his introductory remarks, Judge Henney J states the following:

3. The former Chief Justice Sandile Ngcobo made a speech at SANEF in February 2010; his speech was entitled 'Justice and the Media' and stated the following: "Indeed without the media, there could be no constitutional democracy. The media not only provides the main forum for the great societal debate that is democracy; it also sustains that debate by supplying the information that the people need to make the political, economic, and cultural choices that constitute the fabric of our democratic society".

4. He went further stating: "the media does so much more than enabling democracy by informing and educating the people. It also ensures that the people know their rights and the way to enforce those rights. Its serves as a watchdog and indeed as one of the strongest and most important checks on the power of all three branches of government. And in a diverse society like ours, it has the potential to act as a unifying force and to provide a voice for the voiceless, marginalized and disadvantaged. For these reasons, the protection and encouragement of the free press, freedom of speech and the free flow of information are cornerstones of our Constitution's Bill of Rights".

5. The rights to the freedom of press are important however, as with the fair trial rights in the Bill of Rights, there are limitations. The rights of the accused are also entrenched in the Bill of Rights in terms of section 35. With both of these rights there is a balancing interest that should take place.

6. The public need to be informed about what is factually correct and the media is able to do this, however at times what the media states is not always factually correct.

In terms of 'Trial by Media' (in this case *prior* to the court case, not before, and during) Judge Henney J states the following:

Trial by Media:

33. There is no legislation that governs trial by media. Our courts have not dealt with a matter such as this, where a stay in prosecution was requested as on the grounds as claimed by the applicant. The term trial by media relates to a matter that has received extensive media coverage prior to the trial commencing, this is known as pre trial publicity. The argument here would be that the pre trial publicity would adversely affect one of the parties and would be prejudicial to the parties' right to a fair trial.

34. The reports relied on by the applicant to show that there was adverse media publicity is not in dispute. The Court will deal with this issue in evaluating the merits of the application; whether these rights to a fair trial had been affected thereby, will be discussed elsewhere in this judgment.

In his concluding remarks, Judge Henney J states the following:

I am of the view that the applicant has not been able to prove that the adverse media coverage would lead to trial related prejudice. Based on the papers before the court the applicant has failed to show the trial related prejudice affected because of the adverse media coverage.

122. We will be confronted in South Africa where there is adverse media coverage for a particular case but that in itself can not be sufficient grounds to show that it would warrant a stay in prosecution. In the past judges have adjudicated and dealt with such cases.

123. The applicant was also not able to show that there were extra ordinary circumstances present to justify a stay in the proceedings. The applicant concentrated on the media aspect, and did not submit any evidence to show that an extra ordinary circumstance existed in this matter that would lead a stay in the proceedings being considered. I am of the view that no proper case was made out for the extra ordinary circumstances that would give rise to the stay in proceedings. In light of the above, I therefore reach the following conclusion.

Order:

The application is dismissed with costs

The first concept is:

precedent

noun

ˈprɛsɪd(ə)nt/

an earlier event or action that is regarded as an example or guide to be considered in subsequent similar circumstances.

"there are substantial precedents for using interactive media in training"

synonyms:	model, exemplar, example, pattern, previous case, prior case, previous instance/example, prior instance/example

adjective

prɪˈsiːd(ə)nt,ˈprɛsɪ-/

preceding in time, order, or importance.

"a precedent case"

*In common law legal systems, a **precedent** or **authority** is a principle or rule established in a previous legal case that is either binding on or persuasive for a court or other tribunal when deciding* *subsequent cases with similar issues or facts. The general principle in common law legal systems is that similar cases should be decided so as to give similar and predictable outcomes, and the principle of precedent is the mechanism by which that goal is attained.*

– via Wikipedia

The second concept is:

Stare decisis

Stare decisis *is a legal principle by which judges are obliged to respect the precedent established by prior decisions. The words originate from the phrasing of the principle in the Latin maxim Stare decisis et non quieta movere: "to stand by decisions and not disturb the undisturbed." In a legal context, this is understood to mean that courts should generally abide by precedent and not disturb settled matters.*

– via Wikipedia

The third concept is:

Case Law

Case law *is the set of decisions of adjudicatory tribunals that can be cited as precedent. In most countries, including most European countries, the term is applied to any set of rulings on law which is guided by previous rulings, for example, previous decisions of a government agency - that is, precedential case law can arise from either a judicial ruling or a ruling of an adjudication within an executive branch agency.*

– via Wikipedia

Heroism?

Never a good deed goes unpunished…
The road to hell is paved with good intentions…

Oscar epic journey to the London Olympics started with an invitation – a 'good deed' – extended to him by the IAAF. Later, after doing some research, the IAAF backtracked and tried to rescind their offer. Oscar hired a team of scientists, took them to a court of Arbitration and won the right to compete against able-bodied athletes. By then the world supported his cause, and the IAAF were cowed into allowing Oscar his way. After all, what harm could it do?

We'll start by looking at Oscar's own definitions of heroism. Then we'll look at the behind the scenes battles to maintain his 'versions' (pre-trial, this particular narrative has nothing to do with the trial) and finally we analyse how the media – and you and I – are complicit in these fictions. Yes, retrospectively one can say that is what large portions were. The 'able-bodied' aspect is an obvious one, and one that won't come as a surprise to many people. But it may come as a spectacular surprise – the true dimensions of it – to others.

"I have a strong sense that I have to educate people about disability." These are Oscar's words. In 2014 we can look back and say the education we've had is that we must pretend that Oscar (and presumably other disabled athletes too) are not disabled. They're just like us. We may be inspired by this spirit of 'transcendence' if that's what it is. Of course if it is born out of a sense of privilege (I should be allowed to compete with able-bodied runners because I'm talented, and I have no advantages, and it's fair) then that makes our 'education' something else. Then it is a marketing exercise. And what is the purpose of any marketing exercise? Money.

So where is the heroism involved? Is there any? Yes there is. It's easy if one is suffering from Attention Deficit Disorder (ADD) to see the question in absolutes. Either it's heroic, or it isn't. Like most things in life, reality tends to be far more subtle, and not nearly as simple as we hope to believe.

Oscar's Paralympic journey and his achievements in the Paralympic arena are certainly heroic. Yes, there we have seen real performances, and within that context he has emerged as a champion. Three world records. In the 100m 200m and 400m Paralympics. In 2008 Oscar was ranked world #1 across all three disciplines, and broke world records in the 100m and 200m in 2007 and 2012 respectively.

If we're going to examine narratives, let's look at how Ossur, who sponsor the 'legs' he's stood on to build his brand, his career, and his persona, let's look at how *they* describe their boy. The first and best, Ossur's one and only, the original 'Blade Runner':

Oscar Pistorius is a world champion sprinter who has broken his own world records almost 30 times. A fierce advocate of Life Without Limitations [Ossur's brand premise] *and a bilateral amputee, he is the first ever Paralympian to win Gold in each of the 100m, 200m and 400m sprints (Beijing 2008), and his international reputation as the "fastest man on no legs" is gaining momentum with every race.*

The South African phenomenon has retained his position as world record holder in his category for the three top sprint events, setting a brand new record for the 400m in May 2011 at the Paralypmpic World Cup in Manchester, UK

Accompanying Oscar on his remarkable journey to the very pinnacle of his sport have been his prosthetic running feet – the

Flex-Foot® Cheetah® from Össur. The unique design of these passive feet, which dates back to 1997, has become the gold standard internationally for elite athletes with limb loss. It has also given rise to Oscar's affectionate alias the Blade Runner.

It bears noting that the names 'Oscar' and 'Ossur' seem interchangeable at face value. It also bears noting that Oscar's brand premise (which we'll get to) and Ossur's closely resemble one another. Is this by accident or by design? If it is by design, how much trust can we place in a designed narrative, and also how an athlete responds to interviews. Lance Armstrong is a good reference here. If money and sponsorships are floating in their invisible thought clouds, just how much faith can the public and media place in what they say about themselves? In other words, can we trust their narratives, given that there are financial incentives in place to perpetuate a particular narrative?

"I don't see myself as disabled," Oscar has said. "There's nothing I can't do that able-bodied athletes can do."

His narrative, again via Ossur (in the biography section) appear to reinforce this notion:

At just 17 years of age, after training for only two months, Pistorius took on the 100m sprint in an open competition at the Pilditch stadium in his hometown of Pretoria. He ran it in an astounding 11.51 seconds; the world record was 12.20.

A mere eight months later, Pistorius raced alongside Marlon Shirley and Brian Frasure at the 2004 Paralympics Games in Athens. Creating a sensation in the athletics world, he took the silver medal behind Shirley in the 100m. He also won gold in the 200m, breaking the world record with a time of 21.97 seconds. This made him the first amputee ever to run the 200m in under 22 seconds. He went home with four world records and the determination to do it again.

At the South African Championships in March 2005, Pistorius ran the 400m in the Open/Able-Bodied category and achieved 6th place in the final competition. That same year, he also won the gold in both the 100m and 200m while representing South Africa in the Paralympic World Cup in Manchester, England. Subsequently, the IAAF invited him to run in a Grand Prix meeting in Helsinki and at the World Championship in Manchester, making him the first disabled athlete ever invited to such events; a huge honor.

Oscar managed to shave a further 0.3 seconds off his 200m record at the 2008 Paralympic Games in Beijing, bringing it to 21.67. Also taking first place in the 100m and 400m events, Oscar secured himself a place in the history books by becoming the first ever Paralympian to win gold in all three events.

In 2011, a slimmer, trimmer Pistorius took two further competitions by storm, securing a new 400m championship record at the IPC Athletic World Championships in New Zealand and a new world record for the event at the Paralympic World Cup in the UK in May. The latter event also saw him secure Gold for the 100m, with a time of 11.04 seconds, a personal best.

"I still find it strange, I suppose, when I say to someone, 'Can you just pass me my leg?' But I don't ever think about my disability."

As part of the celebrations to mark some outstanding performances in Beijing [in 2008] *and an incredible haul of 30 medals for the South African Paralympic team as a whole, Pistorius was delighted to meet former President Nelson Mandela.*

"I don't want to be competing in a sport where I feel that I'm here not on my talent and my hard work but because of a piece of equipment."

A piece of equipment? What piece of equipment are we talking about? We're talking about a new – a recent – technological innovation which – since Oscar has used them – he's seen immediate results. To stress the point, prior to using these carbon fibre (flexible) prostheses, Oscar's performances in sport were not particularly exceptional. Instead of calling them limbs or legs or prostheses, everyone has agreed to call them something else.

Blades. What do blades do? Do they run? The typical association we make is 'cutting', and 'speed'. Nike took this idea further and compared the 'Blade Runner' to a speeding bullet, fired out of a gun. But what does Ossur say about their own product, and our boy's achievements using them?

Oscar's 'Blades'

As a bilateral amputee, Pistorius has always competed in both T43 (double limb loss, below-knee) and T44 events (single limb loss, below-knee). His T43 world records in the 100m, 200m and 400m races are all faster than the T44 world records. He credits his running legs – the Flex-Foot® Cheetah® from Össur (often referring to them as his blades) – with enabling him to run at his fastest and accomplish his unique achievements. He also finds comfortable walking and the ability to remain active in his Modular III™ feet from Össur (part of the Flex-Foot range) that he wears off the track.

Hold up. Let's look at that again:

He credits his running legs – the Flex-Foot® Cheetah® from Össur (often referring to them as his blades) – with enabling him to run at his fastest and accomplish his unique achievements.

And he says: "I don't want to be competing in a sport where I feel that I'm here not on my talent and my hard work but because of a piece of equipment."

Let's simplify that to isolate the catchphrases:

I'm not here because of a piece of equipment.

Vs

> *He credits his running legs with enabling him to run at his fastest and accomplish his unique achievements*

Some might say that's semantics. Let him run! The boy's got spirit. Give him a chance. So where does his tale take us from here. Ossur again:

Aiming for the London 2012 Olympics

> *Pistorius has now broken his own world records almost 30 times and is still working toward becoming the fastest sprinter in the world. He has no plans to stop running at the Paralympics, which helped shape the competitive athlete he is today. However, he has never hidden his dual ambition to become the first Paralympic athlete to compete at the IAAF World Championships and the Olympic Games.*
>
> *In 2008 the International Association of Athletics Federations (IAAF) ruled that his prostheses were ineligible for use in IAAF-authorized competitions, but the Court of Arbitration for Sport later reversed that ban, clearing the way for Pistorius to compete in the Olympics should he qualify. His best time of 45.61 seconds for the 400m at the 2011 Provincial Championships in Pretoria, South Africa is inside the 'B' qualification standard for the Olympic Games and is just 0.06 seconds short of the 'A' standard needed for automatic Olympic qualification, should South Africa grant him a place on their 2012 squad. So, watch this space!*

What's interesting is this is where Ossur's biography of Oscar ends. In 2011. Ossur don't mention any of his achievements in 2012, where he became the first double-amputee (but not the first disabled athlete) to compete in an Olympics opposite able-bodied runners.

Why don't Ossur take his narrative any further? Actually, if you wanted to find Oscar on their website, you wouldn't, because you couldn't. The above link is an archived citation, a recording of a website, which, if you tried to find the original, you wouldn't because it's been erased. Google have recently been ordered to 'forget' people in certain European countries, but the internet has a strange way of recycling its 'unwanted' flotsam. Ironically the first name and face you would see on Ossur's website today would be Alan Oliveira.

http://www.ossur.com/corporate/team-ossur

Remember him? Is he Oscar's successor? It certainly appears that way, and we'll look into Oliveira's narratives (and world records in 2013 across two, perhaps eventually all three disciplines) in due course.

If you're curious about Oliveira right now, what he looks like, what he's doing, and can't wait to see where he is going, here's a teaser:

http://www.dailymail.co.uk/sport/othersports/article-2380447/Alan-Oliveira-steals-new-world-record-Olympic-Stadium.html

If you're curious (and perhaps a little confused) where this *Resurrection* narrative is going, here are a few highlights from the above article to give you a sense of our (and Oliveira's, and the IAAF's – and Oscar's?) itinerary, from here to the 2016 Games in Rio:

Richard Browne finished second [in the 100m] *behind Oliveira* [who set a new world record] *and improved his own single amputee world record to 10.75sec, edging Paralympic and world champion Jonnie Peacock into third place in 10.84sec, a new British record.*

The American [Browne] *then declared the trio were capable of competing at Rio 2016 — in the Olympics and the Paralympics — and breaking the 10-second barrier for 100m.*

Browne, 21, said: 'There's going to be more than one (amputee sprinter) in the able-bodied Olympics by 2016. Most definitely. The

IAAF are going to have to be ready. They have no choice. With guys running 10.57sec, they have no choice but to get ready.

'Regardless of what's going on with Oscar, he broke down so many doors for us and we all owe him gratitude because he showed the world it's not just crippled people trying to run, but instead we're athletes; the best athletes in the world. We will break the able- bodied barrier, to the point where we have it (competitions) all together.'

The hasty progression of amputee sprinting, which has seen Oliveira, a T43 athlete, lower Peacock's T44 world record of 10.85sec from last year's [2012] Paralympic Games final to 10.77sec, and then 10.57sec yesterday, could put the IAAF, which governs able-bodied athletics, in an interesting quandary.

It initially blocked Pistorius's attempts to run in IAAF-sanctioned events, arguing his prosthetic limbs gave him an unfair advantage, but the Court of Arbitration for Sport over-ruled the decision in 2008.

That created a useful precedent, but any amputee sprinter hoping to follow the South African into the Olympic Games would have to endure the same testing process, as permission is granted only on a case-by-case basis.

The IAAF is braced for this, however, and realises the most likely challenge will come from Oliveira in the 400m. The Brazilian, already the face of the 2016 Paralympics in Rio, has run 20.66sec for 200m — just six hundredths of a second outside the 'B' qualifying standard for the IAAF World Championships — and 48.58sec for 400m, and is still only 20.

Hold on a second. This is Oscar's narrative. This is a retrospective on Oscar's *Resurrection* so let's stick to that. It's his story, it should be all about him, right?

If we look back at where Ossur's narrative (now non-existent) of Oscar tapered off, we have to wonder, so what really happened in that 'WATCH THIS SPACE!' space? Did Oscar improve on his B qualifying time? Did he achieve an A qualifying time? To find answers we'll touch on where the narrative goes after Lignano in more detail.

Lignano – the sunny home of heartache and heartbreak

Superman: Why did... why did you kiss me first?
Miss Teschmacher: I didn't think you'd let me later.

Lignano is a name you need to remember. So here's a visual to burn into your – the reader's – brain. Imagine Italy as a long sexy woman's leg perched on a high heeled boot. Lignano is situated high up on the back side, only visible if she was wearing a very short miniskirt.

Lignano is a summer coastal resort in northern Italy. It saw some interesting World War II action in May 1945. About 4000 enemy Germans in about 26 ships were trying to escape advancing Yugoslavs. The Germans encountered a small Battalion of New Zealand soldiers. The Kiwi troops were outnumbered 20 to one, but the Germans – despite their superior numbers – surrendered to them anyway. In 1959 Lignano became an autonomous commune.

Lignano is important to the Oscar Pistorius narrative because this is where his authentic *Resurrection* – unfortunately – takes a nose dive. It would not have seemed that way to the world, least of all to Oscar, but on that warm, overcast day in mid-July 2011, fates were sealed. The train began its slow heave towards the circus that was London and the eventual slaying that followed a few short weeks later.

On a Tuesday, over 150 weeks ago Oscar's dream came true. He ran a 45.07 400m, which remains his personal best. With it- well, why not let Oscar inform the reader himself:

"Feels kind of surreal to have an A-qualification time in the bag for next yrs Olympic Games! Thank you all your support!"

He added on twitter: "Can't sleep I'm so happy. Just want to thank Ampie (Louw, coach) and Seb for all their hard work with me. Means a lot to me!"

In the same article, published by Athletics Weekly, the writer, Jon Mulkeen observes:

With his 45.07, there is now nothing standing in the way of [Oscar] lining up against able-bodied athletes at the next two major global championships. The performance puts him at equal 15th on this year's world lists and such a time could also see him not just an also-ran in Daegu, but as a strong contender.

Mulkeen then provides what seems to be an incidental insight. See if you can spot it.

The event has been somewhat lacklustre this year with Jeremy Wariner struggling for form and no one else stepping up to dominate. The world-leading mark is just 44.65 and sub-45-second runs have almost become a rarity on the circuit.

The 400m event, Oscar's forte, had – in terms of International Athletics – become dull. 'Lacklustre' is the word he uses. It means dreary, uninspiring, tame, bland and boring. Yes, we know what the word means, but why does it matter? And why should it mean anything to Oscar.

[Oscar] has long aspired to become the first [P]aralympic *athlete to compete at the IAAF World Championships and the Olympic Games, but given the unique nature of his case, the IAAF were concerned that he may gain an advantage from his J-shaped carbon-fibre prosthetics – the source of his 'Blade Runner' nickname – and in 2007 put a ban on the use of such technical devices.*

After conducting studies on [Oscar] in races, in January 2008 the IAAF ruled that his prostheses were ineligible for use in competitions conducted under the IAAF rules. But soon after [Oscar] took *the case to the Court of Arbitration for Sport, who reversed the IAAF's ban, clearing the way for him to compete at the London 2012 Olympics and this year's World Championships.*

So we see Oscar is so hungry for this he can taste it. We know when the IAAF cancel their friendly invitation, he doesn't take no for an answer. He pushes back, hard. We'll examine how hard later on. Before we move on, the reader's attention should be directed to the comment made below the same article. Yes, that's Henke Pistorius, Oscar's dad. Does he begrudge his son his success? Does he sound like he is holding a grudge? If anything, Oscar's dad — spelling mistakes notwithstanding — sounds effusive here. What's more, he addresses his son directly:

http://www.webcitation.org/69kFzFy7W

Pistorius gets world and Olympic qualifier in Lignano

Oscar - WINNING the IAAF qualifying round in the 'Open' 400m was not part of my thoughts before your Lignano race. We all new that you can and will do better than the 45,25sec to qualify, sooner or later but not without strong competition. I also new it will take a mamoth efford(but you are use to do things extra ordanary), smashing that time was not expected thought, congratulations. To think that your 45,07sec would have placed you 5th in the Beijing Olympic 400m Final, is unbelievable, again CONGRATULATIONS. Next I am going(not trying) to find out what the time was of the 3rd man on the podium in Beijing - to me (sitting at present, happy for you and relaxed behind my office laptop) one of those steps belong to you.
Vasbyt - you can!!
Henke Pistorius.

The above is not a random or once-off case of Henke complimenting his estranged son. His Facebook is awash with it.

But let's backtrack slightly to something else that gives us an insight into the broader context of International Athletics, circa 2011.

Just how *lacklustre* were these 400m races in 2011? Well, let's just say the fastest times [Mulkeen uses the words 'world leading'] were around 44.65, pretty tame when you consider Michael Johnson's world record:

43.18.

That's a second and a half adrift, a gulf of time for such a short race. Now consider that Johnson's world record for the 400 was set in 1999. 15 years later he still holds the world record, and his Olympic record 43.49, is even older, set in 1996. The 20 year anniversary of that record will be the Rio Games. Oscar's best time? Far from Johnson's, but less than half a second away from the world's leading 400m slow pokes. Why not add Oscar to the mix and liven it up a little? Well, we'll get to Johnson's attitude to this question in just a moment.

Let's quickly skip ahead and look at the times Oscar did run in London:

45.44

46.54

45.9 [in a relay]

The Olympic B qualifying time is 45.9. So, not exactly scorching and not quite delivering on the original idea – to deliver exciting athletics. Would it deliver drama and spectacle? Absolutely.

It is the view of this writer that the flaw in allowing Oscar to take to the arena alongside able-bodied athletes puts the focus on him – and *completely* on him – for all the wrong reasons. Has he overcome barriers? Certainly. Do the athletes beside him who must also train and qualify and race – some who go on to win – do they not also overcome enormous barriers? What about *their* discipline to train? Their struggles and disappointments? And when they are in the arena, don't each of them deserve our attention? The Olympic champions, don't they deserve our love and support? Or should we be focussing, during the actual Games, on one man with no legs. Is that the time and place to do that?

The Paralympics are there to celebrate the triumphs and successes of Paralympians. The Olympics are there to celebrate – unquestionably – the best athletes in the world. Is Oscar one of the best athletes in the world? Science and logic say no, not even close. The IAAF have said the same. And even Oscar – as a young man – said the same about himself. If that isn't enough, we all know he competed in the London Olympics anyway. How did he perform at the event itself?

Lacklustre.

See for yourself.

https://www.youtube.com/watch?v=HuR6g_dpxAo

https://www.youtube.com/watch?v=xTdNo7RSWWs

His times were slow and he came last in virtually all the events he competed in. But because he is wearing 'blades', he's different and we should pay attention. Really? That's not what the Olympic Games are for.

While we're examining the 400m, and world records, what is the situation with the woman's race? The reader may be interested to know the women's world record is even older. East Germany's Maria Koch set her world record of 47.60 in 1985; it's almost 30 years old now.

Koch is believed by some to have achieved this mark using an anabolic steroid called Oral-Turinabol (4-Chlorodehydromethyltestosterone) between 1981 and 1984, varying dosages from 530 to 1460 mg/year. Although Koch never admitted to doping, a letter to the head of the state-owned pharmaceutical company Jenapharm was subsequently discovered by a researcher. In the letter Koch complained that a rival (Bärbel) received larger doses of these steroids than herself. Why? Because Wöckel had a relative working in the company.

For the purposes of my – the writer's narrative – and this overarching theme of *Resurrection*, and authenticity, and amnesia, it's unfortunate that one can't bring Caster Semenya into the story as a sort of parallel because she also had her run ins and outs with the IAAF, was also seen to be a media darling, and was 'tolerated' if that is the word – was she? – to liven up the women's 400m. An interesting angle, but Caster is an 800m specialist. Even so, her story is worthy of some cursory re-examination.

Parallels with Caster Semenya

Mrs. Doubtfire: I hope you don't mind me being a tad rude, but... how was he? You know, on a scale of 1 to 10?
Miranda: Well, that part was always... okay.
Mrs. Doubtfire: Just okay? Well, he was probably a Casanova compared to poor old Winston.

In 2009, following a triumph on the track a reporter asked Caster about rumours surrounding her gender. "I have no idea about that. I don't know who said that, I don't give a damn about it." 2009 was the same year Caster ran a 1:55:45 800m. To put this time in perspective, the year prior to this phenomenal run she was 9 seconds slower. 4 years later her best time was three and half seconds adrift, and her 2:02:66 in Rome was Caster's best effort so far this year. 7 seconds slower after 5 years is not the sort of progression any athlete wants. So what happened?

Well, if we go back, the informed reader may recall that the IAAF did get involved, but were seen to be discriminating against her, and even racist, when they tested her case in 2009. Michael Johnson, a name we'll get to again in just a moment, criticised the IAAF's handling of her gender testing, and in South Africa, there was a furore. In fact, Caster became a *cause célèbre.*

If Oscar was a darling of athletics, Caster was fast becoming its first princess. Despite a long period of suspenseful, mysterious deliberation, the South African sports ministry eventually released a statement saying Caster could keep her medal and prize money. But they didn't reveal much about the results of the IAAF's gender testing.

The IAAF seems to have repeated the same mistake they made with Oscar. Though they criticised the performance scientifically, they were not prepared to defend these positions (even though they appear, even on the face of it, highly defensible). Would public ire cost them...and the sports...and all the athletes (as an average) financially?

Hang on. So is it less about fair sporting codes and more about good relations with the public. Is it all about great PR? Corporate sponsorships? Goodwill? Hold those in one hand and science in the other.

By the end of the year the Track and Field News (a magazine describing itself as 'the bible of sport') voted Caster the Number One Women's 800 metre of the year. In March of the following year she was denied the chance to compete at a track and field event in Stellenbosch. Why? The IAAF had not yet released the findings of her gender test.

In the end their findings were never released, but the IAAF cleared her, and she was allowed to return to international competition in July. In 2012 she was given the honor of carrying the flag during the opening ceremony of the 2012 Olympics. In an ironic twist, Oscar was given the honour of carrying the South African flag at the closing ceremony. At the time he tweeted:

"Really feel honoured … What a great ending to the games it'll be!"

But a more reasoned spectator might wonder why both flag bearers had both been banned by the IAAF, and yet were seen as 'champions who defied the odds'. What were 'the odds' exactly? The IAAF? Science? Should the honour of carrying a nations flag at a sporting event not be based more fully on a record of honest to goodness athletic achievement? You know: unblemished. Is it that difficult to find good, strong, salt of the Earth champions?

Because one could argue that the flag bearers in 2012, both of them, were both activists, both political figures, rather than athletes in their own right. Of course, were you to ask Oscar and Semenya whether *they* wished to be seen as activists, their answer would probably be no, they want to be seen as authentic, talented athletes. Here is the first clue showing us where and how the narrative of the athlete, and the narrative the media and public imposes of them, diverge.

If these observations seem unfair or even facetious, consider what actually happened to both athletes in the same Olympics. Caster silvered in the 800m, running 1:57.23. She overtook six competitors over the final 150 metres. But she did not pass Savinova, of Russia. Caster settled for just over a second behind the gold medallist. BBC coverage at the time, citing Caster's best time (yes, that 1:55:45 from 2009) pontificated on whether Caster had thrown the race. The person who raised this was not just any commentator; it was the British hurdler, Colin Jackson.

In 2014 Caster was in the news for receiving the Order of Ikhamanga on Freedom Day, and questioned on whether she had paid lobola. Was she or wasn't she planning to marry Violet Raseboya? At the time of writing Caster has maintained she has no plans to marry Violet.

So what? Well, a postscript to this paragraph may be in order. A comment reached me recently from a friend of mine. She's an anaesthetist. She also ran the Comrades for the second time this year. What relevance does Caster's sexual orientation have?

http://www.dailytelegraph.com.au/sport/semenya-has-no-womb-or-ovaries/story-e6frexni-1225771672245?nk=5f659dee2c4d36ae43e288c8a478edf3

Well, it may be tempting to say (reflexively, and no small modicum of righteous indignation perhaps) 'no relevance'. Of course, when you have an athlete under investigation by the IAAF, one has to ask, why? Who cares? A lone voice at the IAAF? Or does it come about from a lot of voices – from concerned fellow athletes – that eventually become a real issue? Could their concerns be legitimate?

And the IAAF could have handled themselves better, through this minefield. How, I have no idea, but let's presume they could. When the results of these gender tests are not released, one inevitably wonders, why? Let's be fair to Caster, by all means, but let's be fair to her rivals also. No woman's race could be said to be fairly contested if a man (an obvious man) competed against a field of women.

The sexes are separated because as a general rule, males outperform females. The distinguishing factor, besides the genitals themselves, lies in the chemistry of human bodies. At a chemical and hormonal level male tissues contain a certain amount of naturally occurring testosterone, which improves strength and performance. Women have large amounts of another hormone, Oestrogen.

If Caster's muscular appearance, and also the manner in which she conducts herself (her orientation) in other words, are more man-like than woman-like, and if her performances are extremely out of the ordinary, female athletes may rightly be concerned about testosterone doping. It's happened before, to the extent that some of these dopers became men for all intents and purposes, and actually went ahead with sex change operations. It is easy to get caught up in a self righteous circus based on gender rights, and lose sight of the more simple test that's really involved: is this a case of women competing against women?

Why Caster's sexual orientation matters, is it provides an intuitive answer – not a definitive answer – to the question whether she may have an advantage. One can argue – yes – that her testosterone is a 'natural' aberration. But one can equally argue, is it fair?

I think one can go even further than this, and this is ultimately the real test one can and should apply to gauge the 'fairness' of these murky cases:

How honest is the performance?

To interrogate this, have a look at this story.

http://www.telegraph.co.uk/sport/othersports/athletics/6059875/Mother-of-800m-winner-Caster-Semenya-dismisses-gender-questions.html

Semenya's mother, Dorcus said: "I am not even worried about that (claims she is a male) because I know who and what my child is. Mokgadi Caster is a girl and no one can change that."

She added: "If you go (to) my home village and ask any of my neighbours, they would tell you that Mokgadi is a girl.

"They know because they helped raise her. People can say whatever they like but the truth will remain, which is that my child is a girl.

"I am not concerned about such things."

The summary of these non-specific responses is broadly: *We don't really know, it's probably nothing, don't worry about it.*

But, is that acceptable? Is that fair? I mean, let's say you're an upcoming coming young (female) athlete, and out of nowhere, this girl – a very masculine girl it has to be said – absolutely DESTROYS the field on the track. She is absolutely dominant. And...the masculinity is noticeable for good reason. (Or not?)

And then there's this:

The runner's coach Michael Seme laughed off the allegations, saying the athlete fielded <u>constant questions about whether she was a boy from younger athletes when training</u>.

"Then she has to explain that she can't help the fact that her voice is so gruff and that she really is a girl. The remarkable thing is that Caster remains completely calm and never loses her dignity when she is questioned about her gender," Seme said.

"I am not concerned about such things."

Yes but perhaps we should be. Instead of celebration Caster's resilience and toughness (which, yes are commendable) we also need to be fair and consider 'contant questions...from younger athletes.' What is the source of those concerns? Is 'laughing them off' an acceptable, fair and honest response?

"I am not concerned about such things."

Now it is clearly problematic to know for certain the answer to these difficult questions without scientific testing, which is why there is scientific testing. When we are concerned, we accept there is an issue and we interrogate it. Then we find ourselves with more information, and a better illuminated reality. In Caster's case, yes, it is a sensitive and private issue. But in fairness, if you are competing in sport, a point must come when one inwardly acknowledges some of one's own basic anatomical differences. It might be a deep voice, it might be different muscles, it might be different rituals in the dressing rooms.

Science may show Caster to be a hermaphrodite (both male and female organs), but what about Caster? Was she *completely unaware* of these anatomical differences in herself? Was Oscar? When Oscar puts on his prostheses does he feel...no difference?

Or:

were these differences/abnormalities/advantages carefully and strategically hidden, in a resolute scheme of carefully executed deception?

This is a question. Science ultimately shows us the answer. My concern is why we can't get these answers from the athletes themselves? My concern is why we the public and the media and the scientists can't be reasonable about interrogating these questions. Why is there an avoidance to testing? Is it, once again, a case of winning at all costs? That's the psychology we are bought into, so we buy into it, and sell it to everyone else.

And because I can win, I must now insist that I should, and the public then make me their spokesperson, their champion of activism? Is that fair? It may be fair to Caster and Oscar but what about their competitors? One day you may find yourself in the same situation. Someone wins an unfair advantage. Should they be given the benefit of the doubt, at your expense, simply on the basis that they were entrepreneurial (greedy) and opportunistic (ambitious), and seized their chance? Because the public and the media seem to forget the IAAF will only act against certain athletes if they feel *other* athletes' rights to a fair race are being impinged. It's never a willy nilly, let's-do-this-for-fun or because-we-can perfunctory prosecution. The IAAF act on behalf of other athletes. And then are condemned by the public for discrimination. Effectively, by winning the right not to be discriminated against – for one or two individual athletes, we have to face the possibility that these come at the expense of a multitude of other athletes. It's a great story until you or I are one of the other athletes.

It gets worse, of course, when these athletes with special privileges are also world champions. Because then it renders everyone else's efforts as expendable (especially if they do have an artificial advantage, and are competing at the highest levels). It's wonderful to win medals, it's wonderful to be able to call yourself an Olympic Champion, but do those words really mean anything, if the science of sport is relegated in favour of populism?

Another question worth asking:

where does this culture of believing in things at face value come from?

Why is there is generalised aversion, this sweeping apathy against interrogation? Isn't it because we're taught to esteem faith above all? That the more we believe without evidence the better we are as human beings? Just try taking that attitude into medicine or stockbroking. Or farming. Or marriage. Words, certainly, are powerful and sufficient. If we believe them, and in them, is that enough? We're told it is. Just have faith. And what is meant to be will be. It's all part of God's plan. Don't fight it, let it be. But talk is also cheap, and we know how gullible we all are to scammers and fraudsters. Think about it. In a world where people accept what you tell them, it's perfect, it's a perfect world for cheaters and manipulators. Some people *completely* occupy that world, they inhabit it, and they can become incredibly wealthy through nothing more than serial scheming. This is the world of the Ponzi schemers. And the religious charlatans. And the snake oil salesmen. They're clichés because they are clichés. The world is replete with these stories.

In *Restitutions*, Book #4 in this series, if you join me once again, I will take the reader on an adventure into the margins of error. Where we face the possibilities of being wrong with enthusiasm! And that's when we learn. That's when we grow. When we insist on our rightness, we become rigid and stuck, and that's when we stagnate. That's when we break.

When we have open minds about interesting exceptions like Caster and Oscar, we learn about who other people are and can be, but equally, vitally, we learn about ourselves.

In 2014 neither Caster nor Oscar seem in positions to threaten the elite athletes in their respective fields. And perhaps, ultimately, time has mended the situation. I dare say it has been handled in the best way, from any particular perspective. But the issue is brought up here so the reader can better discern the *next* unfair advantage when it comes along. And it is coming along, boy oh boy it's coming. Just in the field of Paralympics and prostheses a wave of athletes are about to come through. Soon they will threaten the world records of able-bodied runners. What then? As doping becomes more sophisticated, how do we become more morally in tune and sophisticated to stay ahead of those curves?

Our goal is better discernment. Our target is a more equitable society and also a happier society – not just for others, but also ourselves. That's how we resurrect our collective prospects.

But to do that we need to be honest with ourselves. Our concept of heroism needs to be democratic and inclusive, rather than isolationist, selective and exclusive. We have to be careful about making exceptions, but also not too draconian that we crush an athlete's spirit. How can we do right by all?

It's true, we all like champions that stand resolute, taller than their peers. Well like the idea of the exceptional, because it makes us think we can be. But if the race isn't run honestly, then we can't honestly say our heroes are really heroic. And winning can't be at the expense of others, winning has to be to the benefit of ourselves and others. Ever heard of Win/Win? How do we achieve this? And we are all complicit in the resistance that persists, to this question. Nevertheless I hope I have provided a few necessarily perspectives, to you and my anaesthetist friend.

The Circus Comes to Town

A circus is a company of performers that may include clowns, acrobats, trained animals, trapeze acts, musicians, hoopers, tightrope walkers, jugglers, unicyclists and other object manipulation and stunt-oriented artists. – Wikipedia

If we need to intuit (or measure) who Caster is to better understand (intuitively, or scientifically) how she fits into women's athletics, the same applies to Oscar. Is it an invasion of their privacy when athletes make their money by actively seeking the endorsement of sponsors? Is it an invasion of privacy when media attention leverages their incomes? The more media exposure, the more money sponsors are willing to throw at them.

We are naive and schizophrenic if our response to public criticism, whether in the media or elsewhere, is seen as an 'attack'. These personalities are pushing their sponsors constantly onto an unsuspecting public. They have schedules and appearances to maintain. It's one marketing exercise after another. They earn millions from these 'sidelines'. Should they be immune from scrutiny, or from criticism, simply to allow their feel-good corporate crafted narratives to unfold?

Well, of course this is exactly what happens (as we shall see). And what happens as a result? A Circus with a capital C. A Farce with a capital F. A Farce reflects poorly on its participants. Because it is an elaborate charade that we know – at face value – is not real. It is an embarrassing situation we put ourselves and the athletes in. And invariably, it all ends in tears.

With this in mind, what can be said of Oscar's performance at the London Olympics Games? And the Paralympics?

In the London Olympics he made the final (for the relay) because one of the members of the team fell. In other words, thanks to an appeal and the intervention of the IAAF, international audiences got to watch SA's relay team (Oscar ran the final leg in 45.9 seconds) finish second last (or 8th out of 9).

Except, that's not quite true. The SA team finished last, 9 seconds adrift. The reason they were placed ahead of the Cubans was because the Cuban team did not finish (DNF). One of the Cubans retired during the race, due to an injury. But the official media spin doesn't mention this. They simply say the South African team finished eight, ahead of Cuba.

Falls and injuries are a *real danger* in relays, even – it goes without saying, but I'll say it – even amongst able-bodied runners. This raises another question entirely:

Should an athlete with artificial limbs be allowed to compete with able-bodied relay runners, given the stability, acceleration and bunched up nature (rather than individual scenario) of these races?

There's a simple and obvious answer to this question, but I'll take the reader through the motions.

Given that Oscar ran one relay race first in the starting order and another last, at the same Olympics, this suggests not even the team are sure what is the best or safest. This is an unfortunate and added stressor to the remaining three athletes on his team, let alone fellow competitors on other teams.

The 'danger' within the relay context was treated exhaustively in *Recidivist Acts* [see the chapter Able-bodied but Mentally Disabled?]. The reader can also follow this link for a little additional background:

http://www.sport24.co.za/OtherSport/Athletics/Pistorius-a-danger-to-others-20110826

If the question of stability* seems pedantic, perhaps too much fuss, have a look at this clip (specifically from at 5:48 to see where the SA team is on the third leg and then 6:10) of the 400m relay final. Oscar, running for South Africa is doing the final leg, and runs from the outside lane.

https://www.youtube.com/watch?v=IQIOyVQPd3I

Have a look at the situation at 06:13. Now it may be easy to focus on the South African handover, and believe, in isolation, there is nothing wrong with it. Actually, if the viewer staggers the video (between 10 and 13 seconds) take careful note of the runner in white's progress on the inside lane. Note the gap between both countries at 6:10 compared to 6:13. At 6:18 it's clear just how bad the changeover was. But does Oscar close the gap or make up time? At 08:00 just before the screen fades Oscar is barely in the picture. What time does Oscar run? 46.54, well outside the Olympic B qualifying standard. Bear in mind in a relay athletes tend to have times even quicker than their personal bests because it's not a standing (motionless) start. Once they get the baton they should be moving quite quickly. This is where allowing a disabled runner to run a relay breaks down.

Can anyone make the argument that Oscar is the *best* candidate (in SA's top 4 fastest 400m runners) when he runs a 46.54? So is all the fuss about putting a runner that doesn't deserve to be there, in an event, so we can celebrate his exceptionalism? Isn't Oscar there, by his own admission based on his talent and hard work? Then what about the talent and hard work of his South African team mates?

Another point to make is the attention by the television cameras and commentators on the one athlete (naturally at the expense of all the others), *every time he competes.* Is it deserved? Is it more deserving than the guy who ultimately wins?

In this clip, listen to the narration:

https://www.youtube.com/watch?v=HuR6g_dpxAo

"…grew up with no special treatment…"

"…some thought his prosthetic legs gave him an advantage…hard to imagine…"

"…also hard to imagine he was able to reach the semi-final round against able-bodied runners…"

"…I got a text message from this young athlete…I held back a lot…I think I can run 44 seconds…"

"…not only making the men's Olympic final, but being a factor…"

From 0:12 seconds in the clip to 1:45 Oscar is the sole focus on the commentator's attention. He occupies the broadcast visuals for over a full minute and a half. How can anyone imagine with this full on global focus on him Oscar himself *not* imagining it is 'all about Oscar', as the state prosecutor Gerrie Nel has said?

The broadcast gives us 20 seconds of one other athlete, the world champion, before jumping back to focus on Oscar. It's even zoomed in on him so we can focus absolutely on his starting ritual. We're heading to 2 minutes of Oscar devoted screen time for this race, the world champion so far has had 20 seconds. The commentator comes back again and again to mention Oscar, and by his commentary you'd be forgiven for thinking this was a two horse race, with Oscar as the favourite, and the world champion coming in with an outside chance.

Author's Note*: The above section was written prior to the defence calling their 13th witness, Dr Gerald Alexander Versfeld, Oscar's Sunninghill-based Orthopaedic Surgeon. Sunninghill provided expert testimony on day 34 of the Oscar Pistorius' murder trial. The section below deals with that testimony. After we've dealt with it briefly, we will resume this race!

What's it *really* like to be Oscar?

Ron Carlisle: *I'm afraid you're not right for this role. Thanks for coming by.*
Dorothy Michaels: *Why am I not right, Mister Carlisle?*
Ron Carlisle: *I'm trying to make a certain statement and I'm looking for a specific physical type.*
Dorothy Michaels: *Mr. Carlisle, I'm an actress. I'm a character actress. I can play it any way you want.*
Ron Carlisle: *I'm sure you're a very good actress. It's just that you're not threatening enough.*
Dorothy Michaels: *Not threatening enough? Listen, you take your hands off me or I'll knee your balls right through the roof of your mouth! Is that enough of a threat?*
Ron Carlisle: [shaken] *It's a start.* – from Tootsie, 1982

On 30 June, a Monday, Barry Roux called Dr Versfeld to the witness stand. Versfeld, a painstaking, soft-spoken man, revealed additional clues pertaining to the real goings on; Oscar behind the scenes so-to speak. Not only did Versfeld (the same doctor who performed Oscar's double amputation when he was 11 months old) – not only did he provide a domestic scenario of what it is like to be Oscar, but also – crucially – Oscar's experience on the track. I've highlighted the relevant insights, provided by Versfeld, as follows:

At home:

"I fall about once a week. Or once every two weeks."

"[Oscar] falls getting out of bed."

"I don't go into the house without prosthesis."

"I can't reach for things."

"The dog can knock me over. The dog has knocked me over many times."

"I can't stand and wash myself in the shower."

"If there's a small mosaic in the shower I can't stand on it [on my stumps]."

"I have to bend the left leg and walk with my back bent."

"If I walk on a small stone or crease in the carpet it's painful. The pain lasts 15 seconds."

"If I turn round I shuffle." Versfeld describes counting 7 separate movements when Oscar turns a full 360 degrees on his stumps.

"I get back pain if I stand [for any length of time] on my artificial legs."

"My lower back becomes sore."

On the track:

"If I race and am on prosthesis for more than an hour...[my stumps] start throbbing."

Versfeld describes Oscar having 'little balance on his blades'. When one watches Oscar

https://www.youtube.com/watch?v=HuR6g_dpxAo

just prior to the start of the race, he seems to be pacing, looking slightly nervous (as one might expect before a race), walking small steps forwards and backwards before the race. In Oscar's race track *reality*, however, these forward and backwards steps have less to do with nervousness or loosening up than an inability to actually stand still, an inability to stay *balanced* in a standing position.

Now consider the implications of this *instability* (as referred to above) in the context of a maelstrom of able-bodied relay runners. Oscar is standing in a small huddle of other runners, all of whom jostle for position as their various teammates emerge around the bend, and who emerges first, second, third, fourth etc is changing constantly. In other words, in the context of a relay, you need to be particularly fluid in your movements. And we now know the extent of Oscar's stiffness, discomfort and clumsiness whilst standing, or nearly motionless.

Consider also Versfeld's contention that Oscar needs seven separate motions on his stumps to turn around. An able-bodied athlete needs one or two. In the context of a relay *Oscar has to turn around 90 to 180 degrees to receive the baton...*

So let's restate the self evident question again: *Could this instability make Oscar a danger to his fellow athletes in a relay scenario, or even a conventional race? Does it make practical sense for him to run with able-bodied athletes?*

In terms of Oscar's natural athleticism, consider that Versfeld has measured Oscar's maximum stride on his stumps at around 33 cm. On his Prosthetic legs, sprinting, this value climbs to 2.5 metres, half a metre longer than other world class, able-bodied runners. And we're asked, by a straight-faced Oscar, to accept that his limbs give him no artificial advantage.

Versfeld has also ascertained that Oscar's "left leg buckled [when he is] putting weight on [the stump]".

Versfeld said he measured Oscar's height without his prostheses (i.e. on stumps) at 1.56 metres standing, and 1.44 metres walking.

In shoes and/or wearing a prosthesis Oscar stands 1.86 m tall.

Oscar weighs 73 kg without his prostheses. Versfeld admitted it was "difficult to weigh him [because he] couldn't stand still, [he struggled to balance himself on the scale.]"

Versfeld measured Oscar at 79kg fully clothed and in his shoes.

To give an indication just how sensitive and vulnerable Oscar is without his artificial legs:

"If he stands on grouting between tiles, or a crease in a carpet, this hurts his stumps." The pain is described as excruciating, lasting as long as 15 seconds.

"He could not walk on industrial carpeting. He had difficulty standing, moving all the time."

The overall picture Versfeld emphasises is an almost constant state of instability and being either unsteady or unbalanced, especially without his artificial legs, but even on his artificial legs, and he would be far more unstable on his 'blades' than his conventional legs. The simplest description of this instability is that he can't remain stationary (whether on blades or not) for long periods, and feels intense pain (not mere discomfort) the longer he stands (whether on his blades or not). The pain and discomfort is in his back and throughout his stumps where they are stuffed like padded socks into the ice-crone like casing of his prostheses.

The instability of the left stump is emphasised because, Versfeld maintains, Oscar's 'heel pad' has 'shifted'. A normal heel on the foot has a resilient padding tissue firmly fixed to bone. In Oscar's case there is no heel, and instead of shock absorptive padding a very thin layer of soft adipose tissue which is very mobile.

To tests this, feel the looseness – and thinness – of the skin around your own elbow. Press the pointed elbow (the naked surface skin) against a hard surface and exert weight onto it. Consider the difference brick and tile and industrial carpet have on such a small weight bearing area over an extended period. It's very quick and easy to reach a point where discomfort becomes sharp pain.

When we take all these aspects into consideration that idea of someone contesting an able-bodied Olympics is clearly farcical, and the fawning from both the media and the public is seen to be deplorably ill-informed. Also, the depth of the 'performance' we get from Oscar, who enables is disturbing in itself. In order to perpetuate this false narrative he must necessarily include consistent attempts to disguise an inability to balance, constantly hiding very real discomfort and camouflaging pain when and where it occurs. An athlete at world class level needs to be able to concentrate 100% on their races, on their efforts, not on pretending to balance and appear 'superhuman' for the benefit of the cameras.

Yes, Oscar has performed these circus acts with distinction, but these are clearly not in the interests – or safety – of sport, not for Oscar and not for his competitors.

A second question must also emerge from these new insights. How does an invalid person who can hardly stand, and feels pain after standing for only a few minutes, someone who can be cowed by a crease in a carpet or a pebble, where stepping onto the margins between tiles can have him doubled up in agonising pain (in his bathroom), how can such a person threaten an able-bodied person? The answer of course is quite simple. *With a gun.*

Blade Runner = Superman?

Gang Leader: Who the hell are you?
Dick Grayson: I'm Batman.
[the whole gang starts laughing]
Dick Grayson: Okay, so I forgot my suit, all right!

But let's take Oscar back to the start of his 400m event. We're back in London.

https://www.youtube.com/watch?v=HuR6g_dpxAo

It's the Olympic stadium. What happens to this guy in an actual race?

On your marks...

During the race [taken from the link directly above] the commentator continues to insist that Oscar is going to 'come on' when everyone else is tiring.

Get set...

Around the final corner and the commentator is still gung ho about Oscar, saying 'he's trying to keep pace'. At 3:14 he [the American commentator] realises for the first time there are actually a few other athletes running. Now the camera jumps back to focus on Oscar, who is fading to last, while the world champion – about to win – is cut off to the right.

No!

This is in the dying metres of the race! The commentator realises Oscar's 'struggling now and he's going to come across last' and the broadcast actually misses the winning trio even crossing the line.

No No NO!

While he tells us who wins it, we watch Oscar coasting across the line, not looking too tired or too happy.

What the reader may not realise is the athletes themselves are watching the big screen too, *while they are there*. But it's all about Oscar. The world champ (and race winner) trades his number for Oscar's presumably to sell on eBay. From 4:07 to the end of the clip, roughly three minutes, the camera remains devoted to showing Oscar's race, and telling his story.

There's also an interview with him afterwards, where Oscar reassures us:

"We (able-bodied athletes and me) share a life that is very similar…he's a true sportsman…on the track he's all game…off the track [the world champion] is a humble, decent athlete like many other people here…"

He also reminds us how many friends he has here, who are also great people off the track and 'true gentlemen'. Think about this for a second. Why does it matter how wonderful athletes are off the track? Or how many friends he has? Or that they share a life? We'll get to that, because it's very important to his narrative. It's all about other people – us, in other words – validating him. If a narrative isn't valid, then that validation is vital.

Yes, it is the position of the writer that giving the flag to Oscar was questionable. Why? Because other athletes are both more deserving and more 'valid'. Did Oscar also carry the South African flag at the Paralympic games? Because what you do when you're graduating one disabled athlete and allowing him in not one but two Olympics, is you create an A and a B final. You also unfairly focus on the disabled athlete, who stands out amongst his able-bodied competitors, and then you do it again when the disabled athlete beats all his competitors. It seems, in a certain sense, patently unfair.

This may sound like griping, until your chosen champion loses at his own game. Which is what happened in the 200 m Paralympic final, against Oliveira. Then we heard in no uncertain terms about Oscar's complaints (not one, several), and – specifically focussing on Oliveira's blades, where our boy cited an 'unfair advantage'. He apologised afterwards, not for what he said (because he went on to have the rules investigated) but for the timing of what he said. This is where we see the Farce for what it is. A sideshow of feel good fakery. It's right here that the fraudulent nature of Oscar's narrative truly manifests and we see – whatever is the opposite of heroism.

And what is the opposite of a hero? A villain.

Transcendence

"I never lie." – Superman

"I consider Oscar a friend of mine, but he knows I am against him running," Michael Johnson told the London Telegraph. "Because this is not about Oscar; it's not about him as an individual, it is about the rules you will make and put in place for the sport which will apply to anyone, and not just Oscar."

One commentator noted:

A track diva if there ever was one, Johnson was one of the first runners to wear gold cleats in competition. Now, with the spotlight moved firmly to the likes of Pistorius and Usain Bolt, maybe Johnson misses all the attention he got while collecting gold medals in Atlanta. Maybe he's worried about a disabled athlete overtaking his world record down the line.

On 17 July 2012, asked whether he thought Pistorius's inclusion was 'political correctness gone mad' or an inspiring human story, Johnson said:

"I think it is both. I know Oscar well, and he knows my position; my position is that because we don't know for sure whether he gets an advantage from the prosthetics that he wears it is unfair to the able-bodied competitors."

http://www.dailymail.co.uk/sport/olympics/article-2175100/London-2012-Olympics-Oscar-Pistorius-prosthetic-legs-unfair-says-Michael-Johnson.html

But what does Oscar say to that?

"Out of the tens of thousands of prosthetic legs they've made, there's never been any 400-meter athletes run under 50 seconds. So, if this was such a technologically advanced prosthetic leg, then how come not everyone's qualifying, or coming close to the qualification time, then?"

https://www.youtube.com/watch?v=eFfvGHvA0g0

For the record, there's nothing wrong with controlling one's own narrative. In fact, failure to do so could mean distortions creep in or assumptions, which, despite appearances may not be accurate. This can be dangerous. Uncontrolled narratives, gossip and rumours can sometimes get you into a world of trouble. This is true whether you are Joe Soap or Mr Bigtime.

Controlling one's narrative can also be a very effective way of finding transcendence, which is another word for *Resurrection*. You – the reader – might think 'controlling the narrative' simply amounts to hot air, to semantics. Certainly it can. But we also know how vital words are in the context of a court case. Mere words in this one can mean the difference between a life sentence and acquittal. What are those words?

1. It was an accident (or accidental discharge) – automatism

2. I was terrified – putative self defence

3. I'm anxious – mental disorder

4. I'm sometimes anxious – diminished responsibility

5. Ever since the boat accident, I haven't been myself – Temporal Lobe Damage/diminished responsibility

But controlling a narrative can also be misleading. Speak to just about any professional road cyclist during Lance Armstrong's 7 year monopoly and you'll find out how, and why. Or, it's more likely you probably won't. Google the word 'Omerta'. Seeing isn't necessarily believing. Politicians are masters at the empty turn of phrase. Remember Bill Clinton's infamous:

"I did not have sexual relations with that woman. Monica Lewinsky."

Except - Bill, you did.

So what is this word *Resurrection*? It has a biblical import, doesn't it? The phoenix rising from the ashes. And note, a phoenix doesn't necessarily have to die to rise again. It simply needs to fall.

Let's be clear, Oscar has fallen. His fall is not yet at an end. And once it is, what then? Will we see the same struggle again? More unlikely heroism? Because the last time we saw the transcendence through this level of tragic despair – the loneliness, the misery – was from Mandela. No doubt his was bigger and greater. Madiba is without doubt South Africa's greatest hero, and a true hero, a real life example of transcendence. Transcendence of circumstances and the limiting beliefs of the society who jailed him. Transcendence even of the society who received him back. Now that's special. That's clearly a man who isn't validated by society, but a man who validates an entire society. Wow!

And it's a wonderful word though, isn't it. So life affirming. *Resurrection* evokes a sense of existence, of experience beyond the normal level. Beyond the physical level. And we do tend to think of it in a spiritual sense, don't we? And this is what has made Oscar's narrative so compelling. Through his physical transcendence ("I don't see myself as disabled") the rest of us were inspired to look beyond our own limits.

I personally ran a 10km race earlier this year and a blind athlete (holding hands with a guide runner) overtook me. A girl. On another occasion, also a 10km race, a senior runner passed me and, in passing, admitted he was struggling, and stricken with cancer. Then he trotted further up the road. More recently, a local club I belong to held a MidWinter fun run (on June 21) and one character stripped down to his underpants and ran down the road with about fourty other mad hatters. Seeing him confronting the freezing winter air, laughing as he did so (and making us laugh) made us realise cold weather is no excuse for not getting out, and training.

In this physical transcendence, of course, there must first be an inner transcendence.

Let's look at that word again and get familiar with it. Transcendence is:

Superiority

Supremacy

Predominance

Pre-eminence

Ascendancy

Incomparability

Matchlessness

Peerlessness

Excellence

Greatness

Magnificence

Sublimity

Importance

And ultimately if you pull all of them off consistently what you have is *Resurrection*.

Now it's important to bring all this back to Oscar's narrative and test it. Specifically words like 'Incomparability' and 'Peerlessness' and 'Superiority' and 'Matchlessness' and 'Importance.' Remember while we are doing this, the title of this next section is *Oscar vs Oliveira*.

Oscar vs Oliveira & Discernment

"One of the first things we learn from our teachers is discernment: the ability to tell truth from fiction, to know when we have lost our centre and how to find it again. Discernment is also one of the last things we learn, when we feel our paths diverge and we must separate from our mentors in order to stay true to ourselves." — Anne Hill, The Baby and the Bathwater

We're impressed when Oscar says that despite having no legs, 'There's nothing I can't do that able-bodied athletes can do.' And we're prepared to accept that at face value. And why not? Oscar can move amongst us as we do, in a pair of full length trousers he resembles us (he appears normal), so why wouldn't we accept this claim, and even applaud it?

Well, it's easy to accept it if we don't think about it. Essentially Oscar is asking us to accept him on our terms, and basically 'pretend-away' his disability. This isn't a huge step for us either. But here's the rub. We can accept Oscar as 'normal' and 'able-bodied' until he removes his legs. When we see that, the mirage disintegrates.

Remember, we've seen Oscar testify about the pain, blistering and irritation he experiences, especially on long flights. His artificial legs have to be securely and snugly fitted to his stumps (his amputated limbs). To imagine the reality of this, imagine standing on your toes all day, in an ice-cream cone like shoe. Remember Oscar has no feet, so his limbs, rather than being flat, are two faintly cylindrical surfaces, not unlike pointed elbows.

It's easy to accept something (or someone) if we don't think about it. When we put ourselves in someone else's shoes for more than a moment, reality shifts. If it doesn't, you're not doing it right. So let's make sure we are.

The reality of full body weight pushing down on a fairly limited external surface isn't pleasant for long periods. Further, if we can choose from several pairs of shoes, whenever we want to, Oscar's 'leg' choices are more limited. If they smell, if they get dirty, they can't simply be exchanged for another pair. If they get lost you don't drive to the mall and buy a replacement in a shoe shop.

So when Oscar says 'there's nothing I can't do that able-bodied athletes can do' it's easy to assume, by simply pulling on his prosthesis, he becomes, for all intents and purposes, 'normal'. It's also easy to assume in the bedroom, doing that most intimate of behaviours, leg length is not a factor (this is also touched on in *Recidivist Acts*).

Men are obsessed that their penises are large and especially long enough, are we expected to believe height doesn't bother us, and in the company of beautiful women, height wouldn't be a factor? Both of these impressions into Oscar's world are cursory. We don't know, and can't imagine with clarity, what all the *other* human actions involved are, where not having legs or feet really matters. One would imagine feet are important for slick, slippery surfaces, such as a bathroom. But what about showering, using the toilet, driving a car, playing soccer, walking on a beach, swimming or moving through muddy and uneven terrains such a snow and loose rock?

The reality is there are many things a double amputee can't do, simply because not having feet or lower legs creates a situation where there is limited information on what one's extremities are doing, because he or she must make do without nerve endings to communicate these movements. Jumping on a trampoline. Climbing trees. Rock climbing. Imagine doing those without feet?

But do we admire the spirit that achieves its own pre-eminence in the face of difficulties and adversities? Yes, it's true, we do. The bottom of the question is essentially that while Oscar may claim he can do anything and everything the able-bodied can do, what we appreciate in this sentiment is that he's certainly able to do *many* things, and even better, willing to try. Can we say it is true, though, that someone with no feet and legs can do pretty much all those things someone with feet and legs can do? No.

Discernment has been lacking in the media narrative, and in the public's popular acquisition of it. We'll get to that in a moment.

"I'm not here because of a piece of equipment." Oscar is reminding us here of his transcendence. His courage. His spirit and his work ethic. Of course, when one goes back to the beginning, we know it was the blades he received as a teenager that was an absolute game changer for him. Was he a talented sportsman? Perhaps he was. How talented was he before the blades? Not very.

The nomenclature the world has adopted – 'Blade Runner' – absolutely acknowledges the man-prosthesis hybrid as one and the same. So, to appeal to the public conscience to ignore his 'prostheses' (he calls it a piece of equipment, as one might a sports watch or a bicycle's handlebars) is not accurate either. Take the 'equipment' away and what are you left with? Take the equipment away; are you still going to pose alongside racehorses, 1.72 metre tall models and Cheetahs?

"I don't ever think about my disability." From what Oscar has said in court, in a trembling voice -

"I have limited mobility on my stumps."

"I felt vulnerable."

"Terror washed over me."

- we get a different sense.

From what Versfeld says, yes, this appears to be untrue.

Leonard Carr, a psychologist based in Johannesburg has referred to Oscar's guns as another 'external prosthesis'. A way to feel more empowered, and more masculine. If we take Oscar's statement at face value, as sincere, we must imagine that subconsciously, his disability is a significant issue. Once again, by suggesting to us that he doesn't think about it, he also asks us not to, and at the same time offers to take on the role of hero, for as long as we can suspend our disbelief.

"Out of the tens of thousands of prosthetic legs they've made, there's never been any 400-meter athletes run under 50 seconds. So, if this was such a technologically advanced prosthetic leg, then how come not everyone's qualifying, or coming close to the qualification time, then?" This may have been true when Oscar said it. But it's no longer true. In December 2012, speaking to Larry King, Oscar said "No one is running the times I'm running," or words to that effect. Larry King's next question was about a young Brazilian boy. Oliveira. If Oliveira was Oscar's nemesis in 2012, he hasn't stopped there. If Oscar complained that Oliveira wasn't in his calibre in 2012 (and he did):

"He'd never run a 21-second race before" Pistorius said at the time. "That's fact. He was running high 23s less than a year ago so you just need to look at the facts behind it."

Oliveira has only improved since. In leaps and bounds, excuse the pun. Fact is Oliveira recently ran a 20.66s 200m in July 2013. And according to Dr Ross Tucker, writing a year ago on SportScientists.com:

*If he desires to run against able-bodied athletes **Alan Oliveira will win a medal in the 400m at the 2016 Olympic Games**. He is still only 20 with much strength to gain but his recent improvements* *are staggering – 0.56s in the 100m and 0.80s in the 200m since the London Paralympics. That suggests much more to come and it suggests a medal in the able-bodied Olympics in 2016. Of course he may not wish to which would be interesting. If it is not him it may be the next athlete but it will happen.*

Wait. Stop. Let's back up. This is about Oscar, *not* Oliveira remember. What we're assessing here is that Oscar's disability is not a factor (not Oliveira's). What we're assessing here is Oscar's Pre-eminence, no one else's. What we want to be doing is watch Oscar's story, following his narrative, not someone else's. Why?

Because:

"Out of the tens of thousands of prosthetic legs they've made... how come not everyone's qualifying, or coming close to the qualification time, then?"

It's not the equipment, it's Oscar. And he's one of a kind. He's special. He's *exceptional*. His resurrection is the real deal.

"These have always been my legs. I train harder than other guys, eat better, sleep better and wake up thinking about athletics. I think that's probably why I'm a bit of an exception."

Transcendence is about being able to move beyond the physical. It's about being exceptional. It's about *not* normal. It's all about uniqueness, and special circumstances.

Oscar has all of these in droves, right? Have a look at these endorsements posted on Oscarpistorius.com.

"Oscar Pistorius boasts all the skills of an *exceptional* athlete... More than aesthetics or performances *Oscar is a story*, a destiny, a childhood dream... and a wonderful life lesson." – Joël Palix President of the Clarins Fragrance Group

"I first met Oscar at the Paralympic Games in …he was *exceptional* then and …and [someone] who the entire world deserves to see in all his sprinting splendour." Gareth Davies Daily Telegraph

"He is *inspirational*…" – Suzi Williams BT

"He's been a *real inspiration* to people around the world." – Lord Seb Coe London 2012

According to these quotes, Oscar trains harder than the others guys, he's a better athlete, he's an inspiration and he's exceptional. He's the story. He's endorsed – *not* for aesthetics – by Clarins, a company whose profits are *entirely* based on aesthetics (i.e. looks, appearances).

Next, a journalist tells us the 'entire world deserves to see his sprinting splendour' and at the same time, informs us, humble journalist he is, he has met Oscar. And from another sponsor, and a spokesman for the London Olympics we're told Oscar is inspirational.

Oscar himself at one point makes what seems like a throwaway remark:

"These have always been my legs."

Really?

Bullshit

"All things make sense; you just have to fathom how they make sense." — Piers Anthony

Here is a revolutionary, even, profane allegation. What if all of the above is bullshit? Not some, all? What if it's all a con? What if all that feel good stuff is not true? I put it to the reader, as some might say, to consider this possibility.

Why *wouldn't* sponsors endorse an athlete who is playing poster boy for their own product sales? Here you have someone winning the lion's share of the world's media coverage; if you hook your brand onto him, you get massive exposure. So why would you *not* reinforce this narrative?

And it's a simple narrative: *He is exceptional, so is our product* (which he wears/uses etc).

But what's missing from all these endorsements? C'mon, how do we measure the bullshit level of personal claims? If I the writer claimed to have written a thesis on rocket science, or a bestselling post Apocalyptic blockbuster, or that I'd slept with Charlize Theron, or could do 200 push ups in 10 seconds, how could you tell which statement (if any) were true?

Simple.

Firstly, you can conduct your own research (Google is your friend). Research is a fancy term for doing a lot of reading, and following lines of reasoning and making inferences, gathering information and drawing certain, tentative, conclusions.

Secondly, and this is the lazy we out, you could defer to 'experts'. Here the critical issue is bias. Because expert opinions can be bought and paid for. So you want a genuine expert who (plausibly) has nothing to gain or lose from communicating an assessment on a particular question.

What are the questions again?

It's not the equipment, it's Oscar.

And he's one of a kind.

He's special.

He's exceptional.

His resurrection – the shining star of the London Olympics – is the real deal.

He should [the most mysteriously absent question in all the media and sponsor's narratives] *be allowed to compete alongside able-bodied athletes.*

Here's another excerpt from SportScience.com, also written by Dr Ross Tucker – get this – in 2007. (Yes, 7 years ago).

Like all stories, however, this one has a beginning, and it came in 2004, just after he burst onto the scene at the Olympics in Athens. I happened to be coaching another athlete at those Olympics, and so my name somehow landed in the lap of a journalist who wished to write a story on him. She asked me whether I felt he would ever be able to compete with able-bodied athletes. My reply was that given the logical scientific argument that his prosthetic limbs were likely to assist him, the answer would be YES. I did say however, that he should consider stepping up to the 400 m event (up til then he'd only run 100 and 200 m). He duly did this (I don't know if I can take credit for that!!!!), and has gone on to threaten Olympic qualification.

[Author's Note: Pay attention to the word Tucker uses above. He was asked if Oscar would be able to compete (i.e. be competitive, or as fast) as able-bodied runners. In 2007 Oscar's times were good for a disabled runner, decent but not great in comparison to able-bodied elite athletes. Below, Tucker responds specifically and clearly to the question (and it's an entirely different one, should Oscar – a disabled double amputee, using lightweight carbon fibre prosthesis – be allowed to compete ALONGSIDE able-bodied athletes?]

Once Oscar's public relations team got into full gear, I received a call, this time from camp Pistorius themselves. They wanted me to state that he DID NOT RECEIVE [Tucker's emphasis] *an advantage from his legs. Of course, I debated this with them, and said that more than likely, he did receive some advantage, all that remained was to measure how much. Needless to say, this idea went down like a lead balloon, and I was not contacted again!! They did however contact* [Prof] *Tim Noakes to ask the same question. His reply was much the same, and that was the end of our contact with team Pistorius!!*

But on what basis have I formed my opinion. There are 4 things that I believe explain why Oscar should not be allowed to run [against able-bodied athletes]:

1. ***The material*** *used to produce the limbs is stiffer and therefore more likely to harness elastic energy than normal limbs. Remember, shoe companies are trying to make sprinting shoes as stiff as possible, precisely to reduce the amount of energy that is lost on impact and subsequent push off. Oscar would theoretically lose less than others.*

2. ***The build of metabolic by-products*** [such as lactic acid] *would be greatly reduced by having such a reduced muscle mass. Remember that one of the key factors that prevents humans from* *running faster is that the brain is protecting us from damage that would be caused by such metabolite build-up. Oscar must have less than normal people, allowing a faster running speed.*

3. **Simple biomechanics** – *a prosthetic limb must weigh less than a normal skeleton and muscle and so to accelerate his limbs would require less effort than it would for you or I, resulting in greater stride frequency.*

4. **Casual empiricism**, *which is a fancy way of saying basic observation. I watched tapes of Oscar winning at the Paralympics and every single race he ran, he was about 15 m behind after the first 40 m because his start is so slow due to the lack of balance compared with people who have only one prosthetic limb. Yet he catches up, running 10.9 seconds to their 11.1. If you do a basic calculation, you can work out that he is about 1.5 seconds behind at 40 m, and then wins by 0.2 seconds. This means he covers the last 60 m in 1.7 seconds FASTER than any of his rivals. If his rivals cover 60 m in about 6 seconds, that means his last 60 m are faster than Asafa Powell and Justin Gatlin and Carl Lewis could ever run!!!! He's the fastest man on the planet when it comes to maximum speed, and that's just not explained unless he has an advantage!*

Finally, you just have to look at the length of his strides to see the advantage. His strides are 2.5 to 3m long, when most able bodied runners take strides 2 to 2.5 m long. That big a difference is just not normal, unless his limbs give him an advantage.

One last thing is that he does not have the build necessary to be a top sprinter. If you put him in a line up with Maurice Greene, Justin Gatlin, Carl Lewis and Linford Christie, he'd look like a pre-pubescent school boy with the First Team Rugby squad! And remember, in sprinting, strength equals speed. A sprinter has to be strong, not only to exert force and power to accelerate his body and maintain high speeds, but he has to be incredibly strong to CONTROL the movements. That's why the arms and shoulders are so big – they have to provide balance to the powerful legs. Oscar is not a powerful runner, he looks normal compared to you and me. That suggests to me that his speed comes from something other than strength, and that's not possible, unless the legs provide an advantage.

[Author's Note: Tucker's reference to build (ie physique) is more illuminating than it may seem at face value. We see Oscar's build changes significantly between 2007 and 2013:

http://i0.wp.com/www.sportsscientists.com/wp-content/uploads/2007/06/oscar-

http://i.telegraph.co.uk/multimedia/archive/02327/Pistorius_Getty_2327071b.jpg

A third example is a recent video (also shown by the state prosecutor in court), of Oscar at a firing range (with Francois Hougaard) where his muscular arms are clearly visible.

https://www.youtube.com/watch?v=5VWDIlSMTMc

But the irony is, building muscle in a gym is different to the natural acquisition, and that natural physique, achieved by those specimens of physical perfection that are the Olympics' true sprinters.

The irony becomes even deeper when one notes the antecedent consequences of his increasing muscularity; he would become a heavier and less flexible athlete, which in the context of leg frequency, this was the very thing that cost him his 200m title against Oliveira in 2012. Oliveira is definitely a much lighter athlete, both in height and overall build, compared to Oscar. We will deal with Oliveira as Pistorius' successor in due course.

It is a great, pity when 'camp Pistorius' *as Tucker* refers to them went shopping for scientific support, they went beyond the mild mannered reasoning they got from South Africa's Sports Science Institute (i.e. Tucker and Noakes.)

So that's the long and the short of it. And so, Tucker concludes, *while I applaud his bravery, I really do think that Oscar Pistorius needs to focus on being the best ever Paralympic athlete (which he already is) and stop chasing this ambition* [competing against able-bodied runners], *which in my opinion is unjustified.*

Read Tucker's full report here:

http://www.sportsscientists.com/2007/06/oscar-pistorius-should-he-be-allowed-to-run/

Interestingly, Ray Wicksell, Oscar's agent – who features later in this narrative – echoes the exact same sentiment. If there's anyone who should know, it's Tucker and Wicksell. Tucker has the science, intelligence, medical and biometric experience with fitness professionals.

Wicksell has his own experience as a world class Olympian, besides his experience managing the careers and setting up deals for a minibus load of world class pro athletes and experience with Oscar himself, which we'll examine shortly.

Personally I like Tucker's use of 'casual empiricism', something he calls 'a fancy way of saying basic observation'. In other words, common sense. Does it really take a scientist, or an expert, to imagine that Oscar's legs give him some kind of advantage? No. So why did nobody see it? Simply because nobody wanted to, Oscar asked us not to, and so did his sponsors. The media played up this narrative, and no one second-guessed it.

A (Feel) Good Story

"It is amazing how complete is the delusion that beauty is goodness." — Leo Tolstoy, The Kreutzer Sonata

Yes, mass delusion is possible, and we're especially susceptible to it when it's a good story. There's a saying that something may be 'too good to be true'. If storytelling is your thing, you had better believe it; readers aren't interested in narratives about ordinary people. They have real life for that. The narratives that catch on are exactly those that are too good to be true. We want heroes, we want to be inspired, and we need extraordinary people to do that. Real, or fictional, it doesn't matter.

Except that it does.

When it comes down to the effectiveness of a *narrative*, fact and fiction are interchangeable. But in sport, facts do matter, especially if you're on the receiving end of another athlete's fictions. In life, facts do matter, especially if you're on the receiving end of four bullets through a locked door. Facts matter more, and fictions matter less, when there are questions of law and ethics to consider. Then this whole thing of 'narratives' and 'versions' almost becomes academic.

And attempting to draw out (perpetuate in other words) an obsolete narrative under these circumstances is questionable, to say the very least.

In this context, I draw the reader's attention to this story, originally written for the Rapport newspaper by Jacques Steenkamp (the investigate journalist who wrote the bestselling Griekwastad Murders).

http://www.citypress.co.za/news/oscar-takes-beautiful-young-woman-to-see-his-racy-r1-5m-audi-r8/

If the reader did not notice the apology appended to the above article (in the above link) please go back and look again. A cursory glance provides sufficient insight into the basic scenario. It's June 2013, a year ago. Oscar's PR people are vigorous defending his narrative three to four months *after* he'd shot Reeva Steenkamp to death in his home.

The Pistorius' are at pains to emphasise:

Oscar has been caused unnecessary harm by an article making two claims, both of which are essentially in the title:

1. *Oscar takes 'beautiful' young woman*

2. *to see his racy R1.5m Audi R8*

Of course, six months earlier Oscar was splashed across the mainstream media on exactly the same narrative.

Oscar + beautiful young woman
http://www.citypress.co.za/news/reeva-feared-lies-could-ruin-relationship-with-oscar/

2. Oscar + expensive automobile
http://www.iol.co.za/sport/athletics/pistorius-buys-a-r3-5m-car-1.1454996#.U6tuWBCSxOj

After a complaint by both the Pistorius family and their PR Consultant (Burgess) the publication was specifically mandated to apologise (on the front page) for reporting Oscar's behaviour as "brash" and "demanding" at the dealership. Brash and demanding.

Brash – pushy, strident, presumptuous

Demanding – difficult, challenging.

The complainants argued: "This sensational reporting does not serve the interests of the South African public, does not serve the course of justice *nor allow for Oscar Pistorius to enjoy a fair trial.*"

This last point is of particular interest. So a newspaper article describing Oscar's alleged visit to an auto dealership might jeopardise his rights a fair trial?

Johan Retief, the Press Ombudsman dealt with that particular (latter) point as follows:

Given the above, I do believe that Rapport was justified in publishing the allegations as allegations because of the information at its disposal at the time of publication *and the circumstances surrounding the reporter's newsgathering.*

However, I also think that the reportage about Pistorius was unfair to him as the main allegation certainly proved to be false. This, retrospectively, *put some question marks behind the credibility of the information provided to Steenkamp by his sources.*

On this basis I am willing to accept the word of Burgess's source above those of the newspaper with regards to the rest of the matters in contention (bodyguards, woman, conduct) – as stated before.

This means that, ultimately, I am left with a conclusion that may look contradictory, but in fact is not – the publication of the allegations was justified at the time of going to press, which later proved to have been false and therefore unfair to Pistorius.

In other words: The report was misleading – but not deliberately so.

I shall not go so far as to say that he would not enjoy a fair trial as a result of this story – that would indeed (unjustifiably) question the integrity of our judicial system.

Why would the Pistorius family want to "(unjustifiably)" question the integrity of South Africa's judicial system?

Additional conclusions reached by the Press Ombudsman to the complaints against Rapport are highlighted below:

My considerations: Burgess's complaint

Spokesperson deliberately lying

The story did not state or imply that she had deliberately lied – it merely reported what actually happened. I therefore do not believe that the reportage caused Burgess unnecessary harm.

Information ignored

I am satisfied that the reporter did not ignore any relevant information that the spokesperson supplied him with.

The online version

The relevant headline stated the (inaccurate and unfair) allegation as fact, which is not in accordance with the Press Code.

FINDING

The family's complaint

Inaccurate statements

The false allegation that Pistorius bought an expensive and fast Audi R8 has caused him unnecessary harm because it unfairly boosted his public image as someone who has "a history of fast cars and reckless behaviour" (as stated by Rapport itself). His public image was also unfairly tarnished by the allegations that he had been accompanied by bodyguards and a beautiful woman (insinuating that this may have been his girlfriend), and that he was "brash" and "demanding" at the dealership.

This is **in breach of** Sect. 2.1 of the Press Code that says: "The press shall take care to report news…fairly."

No verification

This part of the complaint is **dismissed**.

Headlines; photograph; story's structure

This part of Rapport's reportage was unfair to Pistorius and **in breach of** Section 2.1 of the Press Code.

Burgess's complaint

Spokesperson deliberately lying

This part of the complaint is **dismissed**.

Information ignored

This part of the complaint is **dismissed**.

The online version

The headline did not reflect the content of the story as it stated an allegation as fact, neither was it fair to Pistorius. This is **in breach of** the following sections of the Press Code:

- 10.1 that says: "Headlines…shall give a reasonable reflection of the contents of the report…in question"; and

- 2.1: "The press shall take care to report news…accurately and fairly".

The full report is available here:

http://www.presscouncil.org.za/Ruling/View/oscar-pistorius-family--anneliese-burgess-vs-rapport-2490

Conductors of Oscar's Symphony – in B-minor?

Now, let's shifts our focus from Oscar, as the source of his own narrative, to the media, who may be seen as conductors (and orchestrators) of that narrative, prior to February 14, 2013.

Mike Finch is the editor of Runner's World and Bicycling magazines. Both these magazines form part of the same stable of publications (Touchline Media) as Men's Health. It's easy to imagine Oscar's narrative naturally gravitating towards Men's Health and Runner's World. So why didn't he appear in either of these?

On February 15 2013, Mike Finch wrote the following for sportsonearth.com

> *"[Oscar] represented what all of us aspire to: A deep-rooted self-belief that anything is possible.*
>
> *But behind the scenes, it wasn't always pretty.*
>
> *During the build-up to the Olympic Games in 2012, renowned sports scientist Dr. Ross Tucker questioned the fairness of Pistorius' prosthetic blades, which Ross claimed clearly aided the athlete.*
>
> *Now Tucker is a scientist. He is not swayed by emotional sentiment and made it clear that his admiration for Pistorius was beyond doubt. Yet, <u>when we published Tucker's column</u>, Pistorius reacted with a direct message to our online editor: "If you want to give Ross Tucker a platform to voice his opinion, don't be surprised when I don't want to do articles with this publication."*

To be honest, we should have made his comment to us public. But we didn't. Criticizing Oscar was risky and we wished him well while offering our support. We never heard from him again."

Finch ends off his article with some personal reflection.

I remember meeting him in 2007, when he first began to race against able bodied runners. He came across supremely confident, arrogant to a point, but charming and affable at the same time -- the kind of guy you'd think about having a beer with because there's a laddish quality to his personality. I walked away from that meeting believing that it had to take a special kind of person to achieve what he had achieved. And despite everything that has happened in the last few days, I still do.

So the day after shooting Steenkamp to death, Finch, the editor of Runner's World, effectively communicated *that his* [or the contributing sports scientists'] *admiration for Pistorius was beyond doubt.*

Instead of criticising Oscar *we wished him well while offering our support.*

Finch appears to have done the same on 15 February 2013, because he signs off calling Oscar:

the kind of guy you'd think about having a beer with

And:

a special kind of person

And:

despite everything that has happened in the last few days, I still do [believe he is a special person].

This appears to be both an apology and a message of support. Perhaps the editor, still smarting because *We never heard from him again* thought they'd reach out to him in his time of need. I.e. After shooting his girlfriend to death.

It's quite an astonishing admission, isn't it? Because earlier on Finch seems to suggest criticising Pistorius was justified. Now, given his supporting remarks at the close, it seems he is reminding Oscar that they did him a favour.

despite everything that has happened in the last few days literally translates to:

Even though you shot someone to death in your own home…I still think you're special, the kind of guy I'd like to have a beer with. And maybe we can talk about hooking you up with this magazine again…?

One of the sections of the Press Code stipulates:

"The press shall take care to report news…accurately and fairly".

I don't think either of those words go far enough, quite frankly. If they did, editors like Finch would be more critical of Pistorius, rather than expressing earnest (some might say 'ill-timed) messages of admiration and support.

But Tucker has no such qualms. It is not an agenda against Oscar by any means. It is simply a dedication to scientific reasoning. Tucker, whom I had interviewed on many occasions (along with Professor Tim Noakes, both work for SASSI) has similar sound reasoning on many other topics, including barefoot running and doping. And it should be emphasised here that Tucker supports Oscar's efforts against other disabled athletes wholeheartedly. His criticism, which in my view is a reasoned one, is that attempting to compete against able-bodied athletes invites a lot of difficult questions.

These are questions Oscar, in my view, ought to have considered with respect to fair play and honesty. Honesty in the sense of personal sincerity. Artificial limbs obviously impart artificial advantages, and the degree to which these are and will increasingly be made manifest, in the near future, will be underlined in the following pages.

Tucker, writing in July 2013, simply tells it like it is:

"... you have this misinformation from Pistorius, and the media are too lazy to interrogate it further, they just report and allow the uninformed debate to go on. Pistorius' accusation [against Oliveira] *is not that he is cheating, but that the rules are wrong),*

"The decision to allow Pistorius his wish to compete in able-bodied events," Tucker writes, *"was always going to have predictable repercussions in the future. These were unfortunately obscured by marketing, emotion and the incomplete (dishonest?) presentation of science. Allied to this was the media's almost total inability and lack of will to challenge the PR campaigns and to ask the difficult questions while they fell over themselves to tell the heart-warming, popular story.*

When Tucker refers to "incomplete (dishonest?) presentation of science" he's referring to

'selective' scientific disclosure. It's carefully worded, so as to avoid a lawsuit (for defamation?). From whom, though? Who is providing an incomplete (dishonest) version here? Is Tucker referring to the scientists who provided their (selective) presentations, or Oscar himself? Or the media? Or everyone?

I do not wish to wade too far into that territory, but for the sake of completeness, Oscar's scientific case (when he appealed the IAAF's conclusions to prevent him competing against able-bodied runners) was based on emphasising:

1.   The difficulties of the disabled runner (using prosthesis) to accelerate from a relative prone position, close to the ground (compared to able-bodied runners). In other words, showing the inherent disadvantage, as opposed to benefits

2.   The difficulties running around a circular track

The science selectively showed the disadvantages, rather than looking at the benefits (exceptional acceleration potential when running in straight lines, lightness of limbs and many other others besides).

The press shall take care to report news...accurately and fairly

If Finch, an editor of Runner's World, preferred the opportunity of sharing Oscar's narrative to interrogating the positions of one his own contributors, Michael Sokolove – writing for New York Times magazine in January 2012 – did not. Sometimes the press does deliver. When they do, does the public pay attention?

http://www.nytimes.com/2012/01/22/magazine/oscar-pistorius.html?pagewanted=all

In his appeal to the Court of Arbitration, Pistorius was represented by Jeffrey Kessler, a Manhattan lawyer well known in the U.S. for negotiating collective bargaining agreements on behalf of N.F.L. and N.B.A. players. Kessler demolished the I.A.A.F.'s case, and it may not have been that difficult to do so. "All of it was pretty much nonsense," Herr said of the I.A.A.F.'s conclusions. Another member of the team that tested Pistorius in Houston, Peter Weyand, a professor of applied physiology and biomechanics at Southern

Methodist University, put it differently. "They brought the wrong scientific case forward," he told me.

The unanimous verdict of the three arbitrators said that the data assembled from Pistorius at Rice showed that he used "the same oxygen amounts" and "fatigued normally." ...The ruling might have more definitively quieted questions about Pistorius except for one thing — a fissure on his team of scientists, with Herr and Weyand on opposite sides. Both had agreed to study him with the understanding that they could publish their findings in academic journals, no matter what the results showed. Their paper in The Journal of Applied Physiology, published in September 2009 — "The Fastest Runner on Artificial Legs: Different Limbs, Similar Function?" — concluded that Pistorius was "similar to intact-limb runners physiologically but dissimilar mechanically."

That second conclusion — that a person with prosthetic legs would run differently than someone with normal human legs — does not seem terribly surprising. But the paper was silent on the larger implications of that dissimilarity, because Herr and Weyand could publish together only by leaving some things unsaid.

Since the initial paper was published, Weyand has been vocal in stating that Pistorius is at an advantage, a substantial one. The reasons he puts forward were not part of the rationale behind the I.A.A.F.'s disqualification of Pistorius — in effect, not among the "charges" against him — so Pistorius's legal and scientific team did not have to disprove them at his appeal. The basis of the argument made by Weyand is not hard to follow: The Cheetah blade and its hardware are light, about 5.4 pounds as opposed to the weight of an intact leg and foot for someone of Pistorius's build, about 12.6 pounds. As a result, his "swing times" — how quickly he can reposition his limbs — are unnaturally fast, "quite literally off the biological charts," as Weyand (who did not testify in Lausanne) put it in a point-counterpoint debate with Herr in The Journal of Applied Physiology.

Weyand and a colleague, Matthew Bundle of the University of Montana (one of the seven authors listed on the initial journal article), expanded on this last year. "Mr. Pistorius can reposition his lightweight, artificial limbs in 0.28 seconds, and therefore 20 percent more rapidly than most intact-limb athletes," they wrote. "To appreciate just how artificial Mr. Pistorius's swing time is, consider that the average limb-repositioning time of five former 100-meter world-record holders (Ben Johnson, Carl Lewis, Maurice Greene, Tim Montgomery and Justin Gatlin) is 0.34 seconds. Mr. Pistorius's limb-repositioning times are 15.7 percent more brief than five of the fastest male sprinters in recorded human history."

The most provocative aspect of Weyand and Bundle's argument — and clearly the biggest affront to Pistorius — is their calculation that the Cheetah blades, over the length of 400 meters, or once around the track, give him an 11.9-second advantage. That would make him no better than an average high school runner. Herr has dismissed this as a "back of the envelope" calculation, and in his contribution to the point-counterpoint, signed by four other authors of the initial paper, asked: "Would Weyand and Bundle predict that the world-record holder, Michael Johnson, would run 31s if he had both legs amputated?"

Weyand told me that he has enormous respect for Pistorius and his accomplishments. I asked him if he really meant to imply that Pistorius, unaugmented, is a 57-second 400-meter runner — in other words, a nonfactor in any international-level able-bodied meet. "The short answer is yes," he said. "That's the scientific truth as I see it."

In the same Ombudsman's report referenced above the following extract can be found:

...a high degree of circumspection must be expected of editors and their editorial staff on account of the nature of their occupation; particularly, I would add, in light of the powerful position of the press and the credibility which it enjoys amongst large sections of the community...

On this point Finch and Sokolove seem poles apart. Not unlike Herr and Weyand.

Until now this narrative has focused almost entirely on Oscar. But now let's bring Reeva back into it.

The reader will recall the following basic narrative splashed liberally through the mainstream media in days, weeks and months prior to February 14, 2013

Oscar + beautiful young woman
http://www.citypress.co.za/news/reeva-feared-lies-could-ruin-relationship-with-oscar/

2. Oscar + expensive automobile
http://www.iol.co.za/sport/athletics/pistorius-buys-a-r3-5m-car-1.1454996#.U6tuWBCSxOj

Ironically, Reeva seemed more concerned with the honesty and integrity of their narrative, as the link (at 1. directly above) demonstrates, than Oscar. Now is a good time to ask the question directly. Was Oscar's own narrative (ie of himself as a disabled athlete) dishonest?

We may assume, incorrectly, that Oscar simply wanted to compete, and on that basis, should have been allowed to plead his (exceptional?) case. We may also assume that Oscar himself may not have known he had any unfair advantage, and was simply a victim of his own eagerness. That assumption is also spurious. We know he contacted many scientists until he had found enough of them to say that scientific 'consensus' supported his case.

Writing for Runner's World in July 2012, Tucker states:

Pistorius should not compete in able-bodied races until it is conclusively known whether the prosthetic blades provide a performance advantage. This issue, which has been in the media since 2007, is one of the most emotive sporting controversies in the world.

Further, Pistorius recently labelled the scientific arguments as "so weak", and continued to label scientists like me as publicity hungry and ready to "sing a song" to make a name for ourselves. It's unfortunate that personal matters come at the expense of scientific debate, because in using this 'strategy' of personal attacks, Pistorius never discusses or explains what "weak" arguments scientists like myself have put forward. Therefore, this statement serves to outline the important scientific issues.

... Removed from the emotion, this [should he be allowed to compete in able-bodied races?] *is a fascinating question, with a controversial answer.*

The media coverage of Pistorius largely ignores this, and has focused exclusively on the unquestionable emotive qualities of the story, often in a rather fawning manner. This is of course the prerogative of the media, and it is valuable to discuss the emotional and inspirational qualities in this story. However, there is a parallel, scientific debate, perhaps larger than one man, which has been largely neglected. The reality is that the science on this issue now appears relatively simple, and it says that the advantage is real, and potentially large.

Read the full article here:

http://www.runnersworld.co.za/columns/ask-the-experts/oscar-pistorius-olympics/

But let's come back to Reeva.

Heartache: 4 Shots in the Dark

Miss Teschmacher: [lying by the sunlamps] Lex, what's the story on this guy? Do you think it's the genuine article?
Lex Luthor: If he is, he's not from this world.
Miss Teschmacher: Why?
Lex Luthor: Because, if any human being were going to perpetrate such a fantastic hoax, it would have been me! Otis! My robe!

In "Shots in the dark' the recent re-titled CBS documentary we directed our attention to earlier, available here:

http://www.cbsnews.com/videos/oscar-pistorius-shots-in-the-dark/

South Africa's broadcast correspondent, Debora Patta and a team at CBS have compiled perhaps *the* best précis of the Oscar narrative yet. We hear Patta right off the bat referring to Oscar as "once the darling of the media…"

We are told of his "superhuman status…"

By way of inference, we're reminded how 'in awe' Americans were of OJ Simpson, 'so how could he commit such heinous crimes?' Both OJ and Oscar, we're told 'riveted the world.'

Perhaps it's precisely because of our awe (and antecedent intellectual paralysis) that celebrities learn their licentiousness.

But the best spin on the CBS show is this chestnut:

'It wouldn't take long for the two supernovas to find each other.'

Oscar is a superhuman, and Reeva a supernova, by CBS's reckoning. This is the narrative after the 2012 Olympics, and after Reeva has been shot to death.

Are either of these terms accurate? Is Oscar superhuman? If so, what part?

"I don't want to be competing in a sport where I feel that I'm here not on my talent and my hard work but because of a piece of equipment."

So without his blades…he's superhuman? And Reeva was a famous model, a supernova. It was only a matter of time before these supernova's found each other.

In this context, it's interesting to note a corporate press release from Virgin Active, sponsors and promoters of the annual Sports Awards in South Africa. Dated 6th February 2013, Reeva Steenkamp is not mentioned at all. Oscar is though:

*The likes of **Oscar Pistorius**, **Bryan Habana**, **Cameron van der Burgh**, **Jean de Villiers** and the globe-topping **Proteas** team will be joined on the Virgin Active Sport Industry Awards red carpet by iconic figures from the history of South African and international sport including **Jomo Sono**, **Bob Skinstad**, **Doctor Khumalo**, **David Campese**, **Mark Fish**, **Colin Charvis** and **Marcel Desailly**.*

In other words, only a week before her death, "Kerry McGregor, Jeremy Mansfield, Liezel van der Westhuizen and Derek Watts" (subsequently mentioned), were considered worthy "representatives from the worlds of media, fashion and entertainment." But no mention is made anywhere of the Reeva Steenkamp 'supernova'. So, can the media honestly claim that before her death Reeva was a 'supernova'?

http://www.emperorspalace.co.za/peermont/action/media/downloadFile?media_fileid=2462528

The Context of Pressure in 2013

"The more I accomplish the more pressure I put on myself." – Oscar

When Oscar says this he provides us with a window into his psyche. Leonard Carr, interviewed on the Oscar Trial channel, has referred to this as 'performance in exchange for validation', effectively a contract signed between Oscar and ourselves, on more than one occasion.

Consider that in February 2013 Oliveira was waiting in the wings. Oscar's narrative (I'm unique, I'm special, I'm exceptional) was – and still is – clearly under threat by the Brazilian youngster. Had Oscar not shot Reeva Steenkamp, it would have been interesting to study further encounters on the track between the two, and how Oscar would have responded to (likely) further defeats.

What's entirely possible is Oscar, in January 2013, *already* suspected his narrative – his custodianship and monopoly, really, of the Paralympic theme – was effectively over. He needed a new narrative, and Reeva was his ticket. Make sense? David and Posh have had a larger celebrity life post football and girl bands than they did when they were actually busy with whatever turned them into celebrities in the first place. Oscar's best bet, to 'accomplish more' (i.e. continue living a compelling narrative) was to continue competing, certainly, but to take the narrative into the domain of the glamorous celebrity couple.

The irony is, Reeva Steenkamp was an uncommonly conscientious woman, and while she may have felt strongly about protecting Oscar's brand (the 'running 'narrative, the 'inspiring story of the disabled runner who overcame the odds to compete against able-bodied runners') she may have underestimated *her* role in the much larger narrative he had in mind for her. And needed her for. Possible?

Entirely possible. The last thing her 'boo' would have anticipated, is his 'baba' putting her career first, and very diplomatically saying – essentially – that he should do the same. This would have seemed like a significant setback to him at a significant time in his planned 'comeback' from the dizzy heights of 2012.

"Everyone has setbacks," Oscar said at one point. "I'm no different. I happen to have no legs." Well, not having legs isn't a setback. A setback is failing an exam, being dismissed from your work, or failing to make the cut for an Olympic team. A setback is being a top athlete but, due to politics, due to isolation and sanctions, prevented from competing.

Is being blind a setback? Is having cancer, eventually dying from it, a setback? Is killing someone by mistake an accident or a setback? No, these are not setbacks, these are Life Events. They shape who we are. Not having legs is a Life Event.

And setbacks are tremendously important when one is looking outside of oneself for validation. Every setback is an affront to one's identity. Oscar was not only fighting across many fronts to validate himself, but also his cause. And his cause – in terms of able-bodied competition – was misguided, if not nothing else.

Misguided:

- Ill-advised

- Erroneous

- Foolish

- Injudicious

- Wrong

But Oscar is not the only one who is misguided. The media is misguided. And so is everyone else.

"Thank you to everyone that has made me the athlete I am! God family and friends my competitors and supporters! You have all had a hand!" Another quote from Oscar, and another aspect Leonard Carr has touched on. Oscar is validated, almost entirely by external means and, by his own account, also by God. *You have all had a hand.*

This is exactly why Reeva was also so important to him. She could validate him to the world. But she could take it all to another level. He could be validated as a man, as a lover, as 'able-bodied', as being 'no different', and as something, someone, beyond the 'athlete' narrative. He needed her hand, but it's entirely possible that though she liked Oscar, even loved him, *she* did not wish to rush into a commitment with him. And it's possible that on the fateful night, she communicated this, and perhaps even went a step further, saying, 'I love you, but give me some space. Give me some time. And let me also focus on my career.'

Oscar could not have anticipated this. For such an attractive woman, and in spite of her glamorous career, Reeva had been surprisingly cautious in relationships before Oscar. We know this from *Reeva in her own Words*, and she was no different with Oscar. Of course, it's likely that he took the rebuff, even if it was a gentle one, a delay, as an excruciating rejection. And rejection for a man entirely dependent on external validation is like death.

Heartbreak Hotel: Are you going or staying?

The world was on fire and no one could save me but you
It's strange what desire will make foolish people do
I'd never dreamed that I'd meet somebody like you
I'd never dreamed that I'd lose somebody like you

No I don't want to fall in love (this girl is only gonna break your heart)
No I don't want to fall in love (this girl is only gonna break your heart)
With you
With you (this girl is only gonna break your heart)

What a wicked game you played to make me feel this way
what a wicked thing to do to let me dream of you
what a wicked thing to say you never felt this way
what a wicked thing to do to make me dream of you – lyrics to Wicked Game, Chris Izaak

Now it's time to consider Whatsapp Messages between Oscar and Reeva on 13 February 2013, 12- 15 hours before Oscar killed her. The import of these specific messages – to my knowledge – has not yet entered the discussion of the trial, either via the mainstream media, nor in social media. I have found this:

http://forums.digitalspy.co.uk/showthread.php?p=72754535

At face value, these messages may appear benign.

11 February 2013

RS: Baby can I cook for you on Thursday? (Thursday was February 14, Valentine's Day. Ultimately Reeva cooked for him on February 13, the night before)
RS: What can you eat this week?

OP: I'd love that nunu.
OP: Like veg chicken veg nunu

13 February 2013

12h00:
RS: Baba I hope you don't mind but I came back to the house to work a bit and do some washing. It will help me a lot to get stuff done and relieve some stress. I will go through to Joburg at like 3.

13h10

RS: It's a difficult a thing to try and console you on because it's a sh***y thing and you're a nice guy. I guess these things happen and we can just hope they work out for the best. You are an amazing person with so many blessings and you are more than cared for. Your health and future monetary blessings far outweigh this hurdle. I can promise you that.

OP: Thank you so much my angel. x You don't have to my angel. Stay tonight if you like.
OP: I'm just finishing off at Ryan
RS: Thank you Baba. Let me know if you'd like to spend time with M or Carl:) I'm sure you maybe feel like some family time tonight.

Oscar (aka 'Baby') tells Reeva ('Nunu') at around 13H10 that Reeva doesn't have to console him, and also invites her to stay the night 'if you like'.

Why does Oscar need to be consoled?

What is the shitty thing?

Has Capacity Relations advised her not to spend the night at Oscar's?

Oscar invites her anyway.

Instead of answering his invitation, Reeva's writes: 'Let me know if you want to spent time with M [presumably Martin Rooney] or Carl.' This is on February 13. This is her suggestion to him, the day before Valentine's Day. Doesn't it sound like a gentle rebuff? 'I'm sure you maybe feel like some family time tonight.' There's a second rebuff in there, and the 'maybe' is a gentle nudge. Instead of us spending tonight together, why don't you spend it with X, or Y, or maybe your family?

She tells him it's difficult to console him, and talks about things working out for the best. She says 'you are more than cared for', which could mean 'by others'. In other words, if I break up with you there are other people who love and care for you.

Your health and future monetary blessings far outweigh this hurdle? What on Earth could she be referring to? Whatever it is, it's big. Your health outweighs this hurdle. Your money outweighs this hurdle. Is the hurdle…that she's putting their relationship on hold?

15h46:

RS: Angel I am going to go home at like 6. Please stay and do whatever it was you were going to :)
OP: Thank you so much my Angel. x You don't have to my angel. Stay tonight, if you like.

At 16:45: *Reeva emails Nimue Skin Technology SA. She is an ambassador for them and apologises that she won't be attending the announcement of a new jewellery line. Reeva's email reads: "I would like to wish Sarah all the best for her launch later today if you could please pass on my blessings! Reeves."*

Now consider the context of the above 'big statements' and Reeva saying: "I am going to go home at like 6. Please stay and do whatever it was you were going to :)"

It's a quarter to four, and it sounds like she's finally telling him she's going to go home at around 6pm. Don't change your plans on my account, do whatever you were going to do (without me). Of course, if she was somewhere else, at Capacity Relations for example, then by 'home' she may have meant Oscar' home (and she did arrive at the complex, and was captured on its CCTV at close to 6pm).

What's also pertinent is Reeva mentions <u>work</u> again and again in this short selection.

but I came back to the house to work

and we can just hope they work out

June Steenkamp says Reeva called her after her [work] meeting with Capacity Relations, from her car, on the way to Oscar's house. They discussed money.

And as mentioned above: *At 16:45 Reeva sends a work related email.*

It's late afternoon and it's short notice – to cancel an engagement she was supposed to attend that night. Reeva is a hard worker and a conscientious woman. It's not like her to cancel on work. She's career driven, focused and needs the money. Needs every opportunity.

Given that she came back to the house to work a bit and do some washing, did she intend to attend the engagement? Possibly. But based on what was in her overnight bag, probably not. Possibly she cancelled her plans out of pity for Oscar, who, on the eve of Valentine's Day was upset. Was this an attempt at 'damage control'?

At 18:00 Reeva arrives at Silverwoods

At 18:10 Oscar arrives at Silverwoods.

Now, recall what Oscar wrote in his bail application (paragraph 16.4):

"On the 13th of February 2013 Reeva would have gone out with her friends and I with my friends. Reeva then called me and asked that we rather spend the evening at home…"

It sounds like Oscar had his own plans and then Reeva decided, you know what, I like Oscar and I'd like to spend the night with him.

But in this half credible message is an admission from Oscar that Reeva's original plan *wasn't* to spend the night with Oscar (and neither he suggests, was it his). Based on his Whatsapp messages to Reeva, it certainly doesn't appear as though Oscar had *any* plans.

Reeva asked that we…spend the evening at home…

Really?

Let me know if you'd like to spend time with M or Carl:) I'm sure you maybe feel like some family time tonight.

…do whatever it was you were going to

Cecil Myers (father of Gina Myers, Reeva's best friend): "He kept pestering her, phoning and phoning and phoning her. Oscar was hasty and impatient and very moody — that's my impression of him. She told me he pushed her a bit into a corner. She felt caged in. I told her I would talk to him. I told him not to force himself on her. Back off."

I told him not to force himself on her.

Gerrie Nel: "I've carefully noted Mr Pistorius's *calculated reasons for wanting* to take *Reeva* to Manchester."

"I wanted her to show why I, Oscar, cannot go to functions, why I, Oscar, had to sleep. I wanted to show her why I, Oscar, cannot go to events, why I, Oscar, am on a strict diet," said Nel.

"Those must have been things they argued about?"

According to new reports from police neighbours heard the couple arguing minutes after their arrival at Oscar's Pretoria home.

In his affidavit during his bail hearing Oscar portrays their relationship as a loving couple. A CCTV video from a Pretoria Woolworths (published online by SkyNews) seems to reinforce this impression of a couple comfortable and in love. But a closer look suggests otherwise. Not that Reeva wasn't in love, but that the dynamic of the relationship was not balanced. It appears as though Reeva, who was also older than her 'boo', was trying to slow him down. What's very interesting is in the video clip when you see Oscar lean over to kiss Reeva, she breaks it off and then turns and walks away. Oscar remains standing though in the same position.

http://news.sky.com/story/1219210/pistorius-in-love-with-reeva-exclusive

It's at about 0:20 seconds in the clip that Reeva leaves him hanging. At 0:07 Reeva pushes Oscar back. The commentator meanwhile reckons it's what looks very much like a "a young couple in love."

This peek is at odds with the impression created around Oscar (by Oscar and the media) of a confident ladies man. To take the point further, as I have in *Recidivist Acts*, Cecil Myers says that on the 13th of February last year Reeva had not planned to spend the night at Oscars.

"Then Reeva sent the [text] message, 'Hi guys, I'm too tired. It's too far to drive. I'm sleeping at Oscar's tonight. See you tomorrow'.

There's no bouncy spontaneity. No exclamation marks or smiley faces there.

If she didn't plan on staying the night, she did anyway, but Oscar stayed moody, didn't' he? Just this, wanting to go home on the eve of Valentine's Day, may have been a massive knock to Oscar's ego. Was her desire to go home what fuelled the alleged argument? Why did he not open her gift? And why did he not give Reeva a gift of any kind?

13 February 2013, dinner at 7pm at the Silverwoods Estate: *We sat and chatted about my day* (not her day).

If Oscar had said *we chatted about her day*, which is more probable given her attempt to cancel the evening in those whatsapp messages, a question might arise, *what about her day*? And what was *the sh***y thing?*

Did Oscar not back off when he had her in his home and she wanted to go home? Did a simple argument borne out of 'please stay here with me tonight' flare up into something that made her want to flee (aggravating him even more, and in his mind, indirectly threatening his reputation, ruining his mojo with MNET...) The prosecution looks like it is attempting to prove Pistorius killed Steenkamp in a rage and then attempted to cover up evidence.

*It's a difficult a thing to try and console you on because it's a sh***y thing and you're a nice guy. I guess these things happen and we can just hope they work out for the best. You are an amazing person with so many blessings and you are more than cared for. Your health and future monetary blessings far outweigh this hurdle.*

"My parents didn't give me any scope to feel sorry for myself. They were just like 'go play with your brother go climb a tree go fall off your motorbike do whatever you want. Don't come crying to us when you get scratched. You've got prosthetic legs - that's very nice.'" Does this quote from Oscar gel with the little-boy-blue's voice we heard in court?

My parents didn't give me any scope to feel sorry for myself. Do we believe it? Because in the alternative reality is a potential scenario – a motive – for murder. A girl I love doesn't love me. I find this out on Valentine's Day. Will anyone ever love me? Am I fundamentally unlovable despite all my efforts to be a man, a superman? I am on top of the world, and I'm still nothing in this woman's eyes. I hate that she can't love me. I hate that she sees – perhaps – more than I would like her to see of me. If that is his interior monologue, it's rooted entirely in narcissism and self pity. And that is the birthing place of your average run of the mill crime of passion.

There are also suggestions that his tears are exactly that, Oscar feeling sorry for himself. This quote (below) is another grandiose (and superficially admirable sentiment) but is it true? Is it honest?

"I'd like to show people that if you put the hard work in and you believe in yourself then you can do whatever you want to...I can have my goals and I can have my dreams...I don't want to look back and say I ran a terrible race....I'm going to take a month off and then the next four years is going to be good."

Our own narratives stray far from objective truth

"Most men would rather deny a hard truth than face it." — George R.R. Martin, A Game of Thrones

We use the term 'conventional wisdom'. But do we ever stop to think about it? Are our carbohydrate diets, our depression medications, our Westernised, individualised, suburban lifestyles a conventional wisdom, or has this unconventional wisdom been supplanted by a new conventional wisdom? When and how does it become conventional?

"The real loser is the guy who sits on the side, and doesn't try to compete." Fair enough. But is this conventional wisdom really that simple, or easy? Because what happens when a girl tries to compete on a boy's football team, or a boy on a girl's team? Is the issue about winning or losing, is it about *participation* or is it about fair play? What if it's all of 'em? And what if it isn't?

Oscar's narrative has never fully embraced fair play. Instead it has ingratiated itself with our own notions of winning at all costs. The winning at all costs is an either or, absolutist approach. I win, you lose. By beating others, I define myself. Does that square with the philosophy of competing for the love of the game?

Listen to Britain's Iwan Thomas in this clip. Watch out for the sixty four thousand dollar admission.

https://www.youtube.com/watch?v=eFfvGHvA0g0

Did you catch it?

"I'm trying not to be <u>emotional</u>, because I know him, and he's a great guy. I train with him. The rules are the rules, he's been cleared to run. He should run. He should try and ignore everything...I think yes, let him run, it's fantastic for the sport. The problem we've got is it's very hard to measure it. There is no other Oscar Pistorius. No one else with prosthetic limbs running 45 zero.

So we've got no one to mark him against. It's a difficult one, it's tricky. I say let him run. He's been cleared to run and I can't wait to watch it."

Iwan Thomas is the current UK record holder in the 400m with a time of 44.36. I believe I met Iwan once. He was in South Africa, training mostly in Stellenbosch. I remember this very pale guy with ginger hair and white legs. You could see the veins in his legs, blue and green, and just that indicated to me that this guy was world class.

But have a look at his narrative for Oscar. It's important because – as a former elite athlete – he acts as thought leader. We take our cue from him, as Britain must have during the Olympics.

The words Iwan uses are:

-emotional

-great guy

- ignore everything

- fantastic for the sport

- hard to measure

- There's no other Oscar Pistorius

- I can't wait to watch

This is Iwan's case for Oscar, and this is Iwan' case for himself:

Tweets may offend some... All my own views... I tweet some nonsense but only trying to make people smile...

There's something a tad gratuitous in that, which makes certainly this writer wonder how seriously we ought to take Iwan's views. He's a serious athlete, no doubt, but his appeals in matters beyond athletics are curiously…not serious. His bleached white hairstyle is also …well…different.

When you contrast Iwan's sentiments to Michael Johnson's – the British Champion's vs the World Champion's – you immediately notice Iwan's sentiments are both sentimental and non specific. Michael Johnson refers to *specific issues* able-bodied athletes have, including injuries and muscle fatigue. Iwan refers to feelings of anticipation, feelings of affiliation and how 'fantastic' this will be for the sport.

It might be fantastic for spectactors, but I don't believe anyone has honestly interrogated the feelings of Oscar's fellow athletes. Remember, an athlete isn't free to communicate their feelings openly because they are at the mercy of their own Federations. These Federations are in cahoots with sponsors, and these Federations ultimately decide who stays, who goes. Who gets sanctioned, who doesn't.

This is true in Britain, in South Africa, everywhere. As long as an athlete is affiliated to a particular South African federation, say, it might be through athletics, or cycling, or swimming, or football, but as long as one is playing sport under those umbrella bodies, one is also muzzled from criticising them. So, this is a real question, and it takes someone with no vested interests to interrogate. In others words, not a journalist with particular loyalties or obligations to one title, or a disgruntled athlete. No, what is needed is someone else entirely. An outsider. Someone, in other words, like this writer.

There has been no investigative reporting in this area, so the can of worms that this still is (this being the complicity behind Oscar's inauthentic narrative) – well it remains safely buried. Those secrets are still out there. Karyn Maughan has uncovered the tip of the iceberg in her interviews with Oscar's relay teammates (which we're about to get to).

[Note: Special hint to Barry Bateman and others writing books on the Oscar Trial, a potential gold mine of secrets still exists in this area].

Before we look at Arnu Fourie's comments on Oscar (or lack of), this writer should point out the following: I have attempted many times to get athletes to speak out about their…concerns. They never do. David George, a professional cyclist busted for doping, as far as I know has not spoken to any journalists, certainly not me. I do know he supposedly addressed a Discovery Health summit on the subject of doping. Although I was in attendance I didn't hear him speak, but I presume if he revealed any important secrets they would have been in the newspapers.

We're going to look very briefly at this, and we're going to do so simply. Firstly we'll look at one commentator's assessment, and then we'll test the second idea. That Oscar is *fantastic for the sport* and *his advantages are hard to measure.*

Last Stop for the PR Train?

"Oscar is not a cold blooded murder…" – Mike Azzie, on CBS [Don't you mean 'murderer,' Mike Azzie?]

In June 2013, when the camp Pistorius PR train was still huffing, puffing and steaming along nicely, eNCA published an article titled: *Pistorius teammates stand fast*

The article, by legal journalist Karyn Maughan featured a video interview with Oscar's uncle, Arnold Pistorius. Oscar's uncle describes "aspirations" at 0:24 into the one minute long clip.

"If you had to ask that question [on aspirations] he'd say, 'Uncle Arnold, I know I've got a purpose in life. God told me I've got a purpose in life. Whether that is running, whether that is…whatever, I don't know. I don't want to speculate, because that's for him to decide…'"

Now it's unclear where Uncle Arnold, quoting Oscar, stops quoting him. It's also unclear who gets to decide Oscar's purpose. Is it Oscar, or God? What we do know is it doesn't seem to be Uncle Arnold.

"He says he's got a bigger purpose in life," Oscar's uncle concludes. Once again, if we are going to interrogate a narrative to plumb its authenticity we've got to ask: What impact does shooting Reeva Steenkamp dead, have on Oscar's purpose? And can anyone really be so tactless to suggest her death was some sort of collateral damage, some sort of antecedent sacrifice, all part of a divine plan for Oscar to execute his unknown (and apparently unknowable) purpose?

Let's get real for a moment. The purpose of a criminal post act is not so much in question, as the question of how to punish that criminal. In other words, his purpose falls away, and it becomes our common purpose to castigate him. If we assume Oscar is innocent, then we can assume he will find his purpose again in no time at all, and why wouldn't it be to simply continue the life he was leading exactly the way it was before?

But if we presume guilt, whether a little bitty guilty or a whole lotta culpability, we have to also assume that with sentencing and incarceration (AKA jail time) there's not much room for personal purpose. By inference, when Uncle Arnold pontificates about Oscar's purpose, he's really reminding us that Oscar is 'probably' innocent.

If one is presumed to be innocent, is that preferable to being presumed to be guilty? It may seem a simple question. Where it's not a 'whodunnit' but a 'whydunnit' as someone on CBS put it, where 4 shots were fired, and the only witness is the killer, presumption of innocence *is* somewhat presumptuous.

We can understand family loyalty though, we can even understand fan support to a point. But it becomes interesting when a previously loyal friend, breaks with the schema of the narrative. Then, a new scheme emerges, and the legs of the original narrative (held up as authentic) become rickety. So if we come back to Maughan's eNCA article, what she does is interview Oscar's Paralympic teammates. Two of the three, in July, still give Oscar their glowing endorsement.

Zivan Smith and Samkelo Radebe say no amount of evidence will change how they feel about Pistorius, and what he's meant to them and the Paralympic movement. They say they'll support him regardless of the outcome of his murder trial.

It's a good thing Smith and Radebe aren't lawyers or judges. Because in matters of legal import, evidence matters. Outcomes matter. If it doesn't matter to Smith or Radebe what the outcome of this trial is, it certainly matters a great deal to a great many people. It matters, in some ways, to the world, because the world is watching. And you better believe it matters to Reeva Steenkamp's friends and family. The outcome of this case matters to her mother and father, for example, and Smith and Radebe would do well to be mindful of this. This writer would argue the point even further, and say let's personalise it. If I am shot to death, or you the reader are, if we are death, by the end of this sentence, deprived of our lives, shouldn't it matter why we are dead, how it happened, and shouldn't the evidence around our deaths matter?

Of course it should. And of course it does. Which is why, in hindsight, in July 2014, we can look at those remarks and laugh at them if the matter was not as grave as it is. Death is not a joke. Death is not a setback. Death is also not an accident. If it was, we could murder people around us, and saying sorry would be fine. Death happens because of a confluence of factors. Even in a car accident, death doesn't happen by chance, there are definite, specific factors that are involved, from speed, to concentration to safety protocols.

But Maughan quotes Radebe as follows:

"[T]he reality and the fact is that we know him, we love him, we aspire to be him…It was very difficult to accept, to understand. For most of us who actually know the kind of person he is, we still stand behind him and we still want to see him come back and run and do what he's well known for. And that's being a hero and changing people's lives."

This reminds me of Iwan Thomas' argument. Because we can't quite understand the mechanics of someone with a prosthesis, and we can't measure it [in fact, we can] we should go ahead in ignorance. Radebe is saying the same here. We can't understand why he did it, but why should that hold us back from loving him, and why would he not come back again?

Here Radebe actually crystalises the essence of the title. Is a *RESURRECTION* possible for Oscar? Symbolically it sounds great. It's a wonderful, heroic concept when you don't think about it.

Someone faces barriers and overcomes them. But never accountability. Profitability and performance. Never accountability. We don't discuss what's not working.

Coming back and [running] and [doing] what he's well known for…that's being a hero and changing people's lives.

Shooting someone to death is also changing someone's life. Is that heroic? If we try to be imaginative here, and try to imagine an evil villain, the Joker, Lex Luthor, someone possessed by the Devil. What is absolutely the most evil thing you can do, but shoot to death someone in your own home, someone who loves and trusts you, and someone who you have invited into your domain under the guise of these supposedly genuine feelings of affiliation in your heart?

What if it was a mistake? Whether it was or wasn't, even that doesn't seem to matter to some, because either way, Oscar simply *has* to be innocent.

Smith adds, "in court, nothing will affect how I believe in him and what I still think about him. I will always think he's number one. He's inspirational not just to me but every disabled people and any other people who's not disabled. Because Oscar did things that not even able-bodied [people] can do."

It is here where we can begin to become critical of a sycophantic public following. It is this sort of sycophancy transmitted across our celebrity culture which is unhelpful. Why? Because it is delusional.

A promise was made earlier to interrogate the claim that Oscar performing with able-bodied athletes was *fantastic for the sport*. Let's test that. Simply observe this video clip, and think about what the other athletes (Oscar's able-bodied rivals) are thinking, and doing. Afterwards, we'll test whether our subjective assessments line up. Go ahead and watch.

https://www.youtube.com/watch?v=aVo4VdwaAMY

It appears to be a relatively obscure race, with relatively obscure contenders. The camera work isn't that great either. What we do perceive, even though the commentators speak in a foreign accents, is that their focus is firmly on Oscar. He gets introduced in one language, by a woman, and then introduced again, by a man (possibly in a different language). Do any of the other athletes get their names called out? No. Once again, *it's all about Oscar*.

So is this the reality of Oscar competing with able-bodied runners? Each race is noteworthy only because he is in it?

During the actual race, it carries on. It's still all about Oscar. And sure enough, Oscar comes through and wins the race.

Now something interesting happens. Oscar finishes, and sweeps back to congratulate all the other runners. Without exception, all of them sink down on their haunches, or double over, exhausted. None of them are walking around. One even later lies down on his back.

But not Oscar. Is he even winded? No, he's standing, already giving interviews.

His advantages are hard to measure.

If his advantages are hard to measure, they're not hard to gauge by the casual observer. I don't know about you, and pardon me for personalising this, but if I was competing and someone beat me effortlessly (as in this video), but had some exceptional piece of equipment assisting his performance, and the announcers, public and media were fawning all over him, I wouldn't like it. *Oscar is fantastic for the* sport – is the allegation. Does that mean good for the spectators, good entertainment or good for exposure?

We are told again and again, often by the athletes themselves, that they love Oscar. Really? Everyone? No one minds? Because some people outside of the sport, some world champions, are pretty vocal. They mind. But the athletes don't mind? None of them mind?

If they did mind would they, could they air their grievances and would they, could they be heard?

If what Oscar brings to the sport are our limited attention spans, surely all that happens is we watch him run. Because, again, it's all about Oscar. Is that really fantastic for the sport? Is that really motivating to other runners? Is it fair? Is it in the real interests of fair play and sportsmanship? It doesn't take a scientist to answer that one.

Oscar's Myth is based either on reality, or beliefs. And as long as those beliefs – in the absence of further evidence – make us feel better about ourselves, can we really say these Myths justified? What were they again:

Oscar is fantastic for the sport and his advantages are hard to measure.

Let's do a thought experiment. Some lateral thinking. Within a history lesson. Beliefs and catchphrases may seem harmless but that's how Hitler got elected to power. Wait, wait, wait! I can see the headlines now:

Resurrections' Writer compares Oscar to Hitler.

No, I'm comparing the use of unsubstantiated information, and showing just how deep that rabbit hole goes if you don't start plugging it with facts, and backing up your unspecific ideas and beliefs. The thing that raised Hitler to power in late 1930's Germany had a lot to do with the German people needing to be validated. They'd lost World War I, and they felt beaten down. They wanted lifting up. And Hitler gave them what they wanted. He said what they wanted and needed to hear. He was not only a father figure, but as Fuhrer, also Germany's self-styled saviour.

And he achieved all this on something as simple and unsubtle as feel-good nationalism. His message was an emotional one. He shared ideas without evidence. He gave his adoring supporters an empty narrative. And then war. On a global scale.

Hitler never received a university education, so he had something to prove. He was a failed artist, so he had something to prove. And boy, once he got started, nothing could stop him. The World War he started came to an end when America went nuclear. That's quite a result, a hundred million or more dead, for something started on emotions. Something as simple as Hitler telling his countrymen: we are entitled to more *Lebensraum*, or living space. Why? Because we're Germans. Why? Because he said so. Why did they deserve such exceptional circumstances? Because they were exceptional people. One of a kind. There is no one, no other nation, like us. That kind of thinking well over half a century later is unhealthy, dangerous and one hopes, obsolete.

If the above remarks seem presumptuous, or politically incorrect or simply without merit, let's test them.

Do Germans, even today, like to discuss Hitler, and the Nazis? No. Was that rise to power accompanied by a massive propaganda scheme? Of course. Was all that ruin and wreckage built on the backs of honourable, but empty sentiments? On populism, and the desire for more, ever more, at the expense of others? And to belabour the point even further, has Oscar's personal mission not been precisely the same? A demand to extend his *Lebensraum*. A sense of entitlement governing his living space – especially regarding running in internationally sanctioned events – for it to be extended to meet his special ('exceptional') requirements.

The reader will recall two out of the three relay teammates openly stood by him (or did, in July 2013). What about the third?

Maughan writes:

But not all of Pistorius's teammates have been as willing to publicly stand behind him. Pistorius's Paralympic relay teammate, Arnu Fourie, did do an interview with us expressing his support for the athlete. He also responded to reports that he moved out of the room he shared with Pistorius at the Paralympics because he couldn't handle staying with him. But Fourie has now asked that this interview not be shown, saying "this is such a sensitive topic for me". Fourie has been to visit Pistorius following his arrest, but says he chooses to support him away from the public eye.

It would be interesting to get an update, a year later, on these statements.

It would be interesting, also, to hear the views of Oscar's able-bodied relay teammates. But don't hold your breath.

Is it a Conspiracy?

"You can't get away from yourself by moving from one place to another." — Ernest Hemingway, The Sun Also Rises

I don't like that word. I prefer another word. 'Scheme.' But you get what I mean. And as we all know, schemes abound. There are schemers in government, in politics, your average businessman and car guard is a schemer. Marketing is scheming. Some schemes have staggering support structures. Some schemes, when uncovered, topple governments, bankrupt banks, lay waste to untold thousands of lives. There are Ponzi schemers. There are the mafia. And then there's professional sport. Oh, but there couldn't possibly be schemers here! It's all about fair play, isn't it? Well, is it?

The Secret Race is a seminal example of the degree of complicity that can and does exist between professional athletes at the highest levels of world sport, complicity between sponsors, international federations, the media, race organisers and the public. But what the hell is all of this cloak and dagger stuff for? What is the fuss about? Want an answer? Here it is. It's about money, at the end of the day. Is it really so surprising when this happens:

http://www.iol.co.za/sport/cycling/impey-drops-doping-bombshell-1.1713168#.U7TPpZSSySo

I have an article in this year's Tour de France magazine, a feature on Daryl Impey. It's a biography of his long journey to the top. I feel awkward and embarrassed (should I be), that my name is connected to a guy who – whilst occupying the cover of Tour De France 2014 magazine, now won't even ride it. It makes a mockery of my work, it basically invalidates my narrative. Of course, my disappointment must be small fry compared to the shockwaves going through South African cyclists, and other Tour de France teams.

Impey was our boy to watch. Now there's just Froome. And inevitably one has to wonder, every time there is an astonishing performance, was it...natural...or was there some artificial advantage? If we can be so sensitive to this in professional cycling, where doping is invisible, but the performance is not, why are we so blind when we see an obviously unnatural performance. We're not astonished by these blades as much as morbidly curious.

Once, whilst researching an article on Lance Armstrong (a former Radioshack teammate) for GQ magazine – Lance had recently been outed by Tyler Hamilton through his award winning bestseller *The Secret Race* – I specifically contacted Impey to talk about doping. Impey said to me, "I'm happy to talk to you, as long as it's not about Armstrong, and as long as it's not about doping." So I said, "I'm interested in your performances of late but, yes, I'd like to touch on it we can." But of course we never did.

What *other* point is there to the elaborate behind the scenes machinations that are all our schemes? Sex, maybe. Revenge, sometimes. Power, possibly. Money? Always.

Why is it everyone can keep such a tight lid on these secrets? Because everyone is invested. The only reason Hamilton, who I have also interviewed, told his story as he did was because he was *already* a pariah. Pro cycling had kicked him out, and his wife had divorced him. He was retired. He had nothing to lose. When you find someone like that an authentic narrative finally emerges. The underlying bullshit below the creamy stuff that floats to the top; the hot black stuff below the frothy, meaningless crap that gets recycled by the media, that shit is *truly* epic.

Christopher Keyes from Outside magazine touches on its scale and scope here:

It's hard to describe the impact of The **Secret Race** *by boiling it down to seven or eight shocking anecdotes. The book delivers them—make no mistake—but its real power comes from Hamilton's unprecedented attempt at full disclosure. And I mean full. The book is the Holy Grail for disillusioned cycling fans in search of answers. In a taut 268 pages, Hamilton confidently and systematically destroys any sense that there was ever any chance of cleaning up cycling in the early 2000s, revealing the sport's powerful and* *elaborate doping infrastructure. He's like a retiring magician who has decided to let the public in on the profession's most guarded techniques.*

The Secret Race also achieves something else. It slays a narrative that Armstrong worked years, and accumulated tens of millions, to fabricate.

Here's the reality: **The Secret Race** *isn't just a game changer for the Lance Armstrong myth. It's the game ender. No one can read this book with an open mind and still credibly believe that Armstrong didn't dope. It's impossible. That doesn't change the fact that he survived cancer and helped millions of people through Livestrong, but the myth of the clean-racing hero who came back from the dead is, well, dead.*

http://www.outsideonline.com/outdoor-adventure/media/books/Keyes-hamilton-the-secret-race.html

Just because a hundred newspapers and magazines are selling the same bullshit, doesn't make the bullshit genuine. But it does make the lone authentic voice stand out, and that's how it earns the 'seminal' moniker. What is seminal?

- Determining

- Influential

- Definitive

In essence what a seminal account does is reshape, refine, resurrect a narrative and then shape it into something else, something truer than the original. This is, in part, the intentional of this particular narrative, and others in this series. Before a definitive account is accepted, however, it is easy to heap scorn on what may appear as a minority of dissenters. Tucker, Weyand, Johnson...when there are masses of support churning, and on the decks of those ships churning on this inauthentic ocean is a lot of money.

Note to the reader:

This was sufficient. On July 1, 2014 I had all the material I felt was necessary for *RESURRECTION*. The manuscript had been edited, and I was about to throw it into the ether. But then Barry Roux did the unthinkable. He called Oscar's agent, and via Peet Van Zyl's testimony, opened the door (and a Pandora's Box) to *character evidence*.

Even Gerrie Nel said: "I never expected this to happen today." I'm not sure if anyone did. Let's face it, Kenny Oldwage had gone MIA from Oscar's counsel (hadn't he?) and it didn't look like *any* of Oscar's expert witnesses did anything to help his case. Neither did the evaluation, which has turned out to be little more than a false alarm.

On July 1st one could be forgiven for asking:

Does Oscar's defence team have any ammunition to fire back at the state at all? Can the defence get any worse?

Evidently, it could!

As such, I have added three additional chapters ahead of the last (Conclusions).

The first is intended to build up background based on the new information (and might feel like tired territory we've already covered), the second section deals with two absolutely vital pieces of evidence (dates and intentions). I also want to briefly cover the Jonathan McEvoy article (the 'British journalist) Nel refers to, in order to briefly demonstrate Van Zyl's trustworthiness (?) on the witness stand.

Finally, once these two six inch nails have been hammered firmly into the meranti, we can – for the first time, wave aside the smoke and mirrors and take an unfettered look at *Motive*.

"Did he involve her in his career?"

"The boys with their feet on the desks know that the easiest murder case in the world to break is the one somebody tried to get very cute with; the one that really bothers them is the murder somebody only thought of two minutes before he pulled it off." – Raymond Chandler

Barry Roux really stepped into it when he asked Peet van Zyl, Oscar's former agent (manager, representative whatever) at 11:01 on Day 35 of the trial (1 July 2014) this seemingly harmless question:

"Did he involve her in his career?"

Let's be clear what Roux is actually asking here. The real question is this:

"Did Oscar Pistorius involve Reeva Steenkamp in his career?"

Peet Van Zyl answers: "Yes."

Let's pause for a second on what this question actually implies. Here it is:

"Did Oscar Pistorius want to involve Reeva Steenkamp in his career?"

His agent, his manager (the man in charge of Oscar's business dealings, his contracts, his brand ambassadorial duties) tells us, "Yes."

Note, the question isn't: "Did Oscar want to involve Reeva in his life, or did he want to be in a relationship with her?" Or, "Was he serious about Reeva." Or even, "Did he love Reeva Steenkamp?" It's:

"Did he involve her in his career?"

This is quite different. As we will see, it is an absolutely critical concession by the defence. And, in my view, a foolish one to volunteer in this murder trial. Because if we are evaluating Oscar's intentions, which seem clearly strategic (why after all, should he involve Reeva in his *career*?) then we must also ponder Reeva's intentions. Bear in mind both Oscar and Reeva are brand ambassadors. Bear in mind both of them have obligations to different sets of brands, must attend various events and must portray a particular image (or persona). Now it's time to ask a second critical question.

Did Reeva Steenkamp want to involve herself in his career? Remember, she also had *her* career, which we know was very important to her. She was very invested in it. Reeva had begged a PR company to take her in, and her brand (and brand portfolio) were doing particularly well in the run-up to her first meeting with Oscar, on that fateful November day on the Kyalami race track (on 4 November 2012).

Who could answer this question – whether she wanted to be involved in Oscar's career – since Reeva is not here to answer herself? Well, Oscar, for one. But let's not go there just yet (but we will get there in due course). Capacity Relations is the first logical port of call to find our evidence. But there's a third option. It's Reeva's (and for that matter Oscar's) social media timelines.

Since I have already compiled a thorough narrative from Reeva's Facebook timeline (see *Reeva in her own Words*), I will not repeat that particular narrative here. Instead, I will concentrate on Oscar and Reeva's twitterstreams, and see how these reveal their true intentions towards each other, both in terms of their relationship, but more significantly, in terms of the way they *separately* executed their brand ambassadorial obligations.

Let's deal with their twitterstreams first, and then come back to look at the impact Capacity Relations exerted on their client.

[Note: A summary of the twitterstream is provided below for the more impatient reader.]

In keeping with the idea (first expressed on CBS's 48 hours show) of 'two supernovas destined to find each other', it may be tempting to record Reeva Steemkamp's twitter following as it is today.

@ReevaSteenkamp 39,445 followers (as at 1 July 2014)

@OscarPistorius 351,721 followers (as at 1July 2014).

Supernovas? The disgraced cyclist Lance Armstrong has 4 million....correction...now down to 3.84 million followers. And the reality is, Reeva had only around 3000 followers at the time of her death.

http://www.georgianewsday.com/news/regional/150355-oscar-pistorius-charged-with-murder-after-he-accidentally-shot-dead-reeva-steenkamp.html

It's important to note then, that in the scheme of things, whilst doing fairly well, Reeva was still virtually unknown in South Africa. (Reeva Steenkamp and I were friends on Facebook, but I was – sadly – only aware of this connection after her death).

Reeva's Twitterstream

31 Dec 2012 I've learnt many valuable lessons this year. Thank you 2012 for the education! Above all, "trust your inner voice" stands out for me. #2013

Oscar's Twitterstream

3:52 AM - 31 Dec 2012 In 2013 Ill be the strongest and fastest I've ever been, find ways to train harder, recover quicker and eat healthier! Strive to be #1!

Reeva's Twitterstream

31 Dec 2012 Going to miss some of my best people tonight **@OscarPistorius** @gi_myers @Iamfomo Have the most amazing night crazies! Send piccies :)

2 Jan 2013 Catching some Summer rays. Good company. Cocktails. The perfect way to end the holidays.

3 Jan 2013 The chauffeurs in Cape Town hey. Nice! http://instagr.am/p/UBZZG0wPV5/

4 Jan 2013 Shimmy Beach Club! Tooooo much food!!! Amazing holiday :) **@OscarPistorius** @thesamlet @daytonagroup @haydengiger

Oscar's Twitterstream

6 Jan 2013 In Kalk Bay over looking the sea. @NicAdendorff @AngieS_1985 **@reevasteenkamp** @LeeSte_ens :)

11 Jan 2013 #memories :) "**@reevasteenkamp**: Road tripping with **@OscarPistorius** showing @martynrooney our amazing country! #WelcometoSouthAfrica"

Reeva's Twitterstream

10 Jan 2013 Visiting **my boo** on set. He shoots more than me! I need to up my game!!! #manonfire

11 Jan 2013 #FF @NimueSkinSA for flawless skin. Honestly the most amazing brand on the market - my skin has never been so healthy! 3 years committed.

11 Jan 2013 #FF The salon that keeps my hair looking beautiful @PulseSalonSA - ask for the genius colourist @Jenna_G6 !!!!

11 Jan 2013#FF @CapacityR They honestly organise SA's most prestigious events and manage our top talent. No red carpet is complete without them!

11 Jan 2013#FF @SandtonMini I wouldn't buy a Mini anywhere else. The pimp experts for your special little car :)

Oscar's Twitterstream

12 Jan 2013 Spent the afternoon sleeping on the grass and swimming with @AimeePistorius @MartynRooney and @reevasteenkamp. :)

Reeva's Twitterstream

15 Jan 2013 "@NimueSkinSA: was so lovely to have Reeva at our offices now. What an awesome person." I can't wait to play with my new products later :)

15 Jan 2013 Birds of a feather flock together

18 Jan 2013 " You built your walls so high, no one could climb it. But I'm gonna try boy ... Would you let me see beneath your beautiful ... "

19 Jan 2013 My new apartment will have one of these guys in it.... http://instagr.am/p/UrK8zewPbw/

23 Jan 2013 Learnt about what goes into @NimueSkinSA products this week! Nimue can truly do so much for the improvement of your skin! #skinhealth

Reeva's Twitterstream

27 Jan 2013 Some of my favourite people. @oscarpistorius @gi_myers @iamfomo @thesamlet @thefrisco_kid beatrixleopold http://instagr.am/p/U_4G76wPYt/

Oscar's Twitterstream

[RETWEETED]:

26 Jan 2013 For I am with you, & no one is going to attack & harm you, because I have many people in this city. -Acts 18:10

Reeva's Twitterstream

1 Feb 2013 #FF @NimueSkinSA for a skincare range that REALLY works wonders! My product for Jan: the Stemplex Serum Booster! WOW!

Oscar's Twitterstream

[Retweet]: 1 Feb 2013 ;)"@reevasteenkamp: He certainly doesn't need more followers but he's beautiful to look at & says some smart stuff too.pic.twitter.com/eCLHTYcS"

7 Feb 2013 Blessed to be here at the #VASIA2013 amongst some of the worlds finest Cricketers @ABdeVilliers17 @faf1307 @amlahash and Dr Ali Bacher.

7 Feb 2013 Great company tonight at the #VASIA13 with @VictorMatfield @BobSkinstad @Nickbeyond @Cameronvdburgh @bryanhabana @roxyburger @KerryMcGregor

Reeva's Twitterstream

7 Feb 2013 With my girl @pearlthusi at the @tropikaiot5 launch this morning at the #MunroHotel http://instagr.am/p/Vbmo2cwPYf/

7 Feb 2013 Great night catching up with @ImariVisser @CaraFerns @Fixsacious @StaceHolland #Girls #Event #VAISA2013 #GorgeousLadies7:23 PM

8 Feb 2013 Before you lift a pen or raise your voice to criticise, acknowledge people's circumstances. You don't know their struggles. Their journey.

9 Feb 2013 It's the last supper with @MartynRooney :(I think @OscarPistorius and I will kidnap you forever!!!!

Oscar's Twitterstream

10 Feb 2013 Finished watching the 8pm movie on @mnetmovies to end the weekend but the house is way to quiet without @MartynRooney! #homealoneblues

11 Feb 2013 1 month till my first race of 2013.. Can't wait to burn it up! http://instagr.am/p/VmN_8_oR2T/

11 Feb via Whatsapp:

RS: **I'm always on your side and pro-you and your career, but mostly pro-us and the health of our relationship. We are important to me.**
Lots of hugs. I hope you have a super blessed day. I have said a small prayer for both of us. xxx
OP: Thank you so much for being strong my Angel. **That message meant a lot to me.** I am taking your advice. Just sent a host of emails. Trying to take control of my admin. Miss you. x

16h00:

OP: Come visit me.
RS: If I knew you were just chilling, I would have gone to you hours ago.

RS: Baby can I cook for you on **Thursday?** (Would have been Valentine's Day)
RS: What can you eat this week?
OP: I'd love that nunu.

OP: Like veg chicken veg nunu

between 16h00 and 16h30:

OP: Ok my angel, thinking of you.xx

around 22h00:

RS: Bubooooo
OP: Baabooo
RS: I misssss youuuu
OP: I miss youuu tooooo
OP: I miss you one more than you miss me always
RS: Impossible

22h43:

OP: Yes night night baba.
RS: xx Ok night
RS: xxxxx
RS: I wish you were here cuddling me
OP: I miss you so

RS: I'm sorry I'm not there Angel
RS: I'll be there in my heart and mind xx

12 February 2013

10h27 (Roux says the couple was referring to each other in the third person.)

RS: See your woman told you that you're looking good.
RS: Now we just got to get your a** down to 52s again
OP: I'm missing her today. She makes my heart happy.
RS: You make her everything happy

Reeva's Tweets

11 Feb 2013 "@Zalebs: *Photos* The Virgin Active Sports Awards 2013 took place last week. See who was there! http://bit.ly/VORNdM

13 Feb 2013 It's a beautiful day!Make things happen.Starting my day off with a yummy healthy shake **from my boo :)**

13 February 2013 via Whatsapp [yes, revisited]

13h10

RS: **It's a difficult a thing to try and console you on because it's a sh***y thing** and you're a nice guy. I guess these things happen and **we can just hope they work out for the best**. You are an amazing person with so many blessings and you are more than cared for. Your health and **future monetary blessings far outweigh this hurdle**. I can promise you that.

15h21

RS: Thank you Baba. Let me know if you'd like to spend time with M or Carl:) I'm sure you maybe feel like some family time tonight.

At 16:45 Reeva emails Nimue Skin Technology SA. She is an ambassador for them and apologises that she won't be attending the announcement of a new jewellery line.

Summary of this Twitterstream + Whatsapps:

1. On 19 January 2013 Reeva reveals plans to move into a new apartment. [Recall that Oscar also testified about his intention to move to Johannesburg to be closer to Reeva]

2. Both Reeva and Oscar mention one another casually across social media, but the tone is somewhat restrained. In contrast, both are more effusive towards their personal and mutual, and rarely openly affectionate towards each other. In the latter, **Reeva is more obviously affectionate to Oscar in public**, and on at least two occasions publishes photos of him, calling him 'smart, sexy and beautiful'. **Oscar – at least in public – does not repay Reeva the same compliments.**

3. Note on **7 February** (also highlighted across the two streams above in bold) both attend the Virgin Active Sport Industry Awards.**[#VAISA2013]** The two attend the awards as a couple, and are photographed together posing outside [some of the last public photos of the two together in public]. Curiously, though both endorse very many of their companions, and both post several photos of their celebrity companions to Instagram, neither mentions the other – at all! This seems to be a conscious effort at least on February 7 to sequestrate both their brands and careers. But where would such a strategic intentionality originate?

4. Notice how heavily invested Reeva is in promoting **Nimue**. She promotes other brands too [the tweets above are obviously a small selection of more relevant tweets], but Nimue is definitely a top priority.

5. Notice also that there is a distinct change of tone from the blubbering booboos and baabaas and many touching terms of endearment on the 11th and 12th to the slight standoffishness on the 13th. Reeva has suggested cooking him dinner on the 14th, but balks at sleeping over on the 13th, suggesting to Oscar to 'maybe' spend time with his family. As mentioned earlier in this narrative, something 'shitty' has come up on the 13th.

6. The reader will recall that at **16:45**: Reeva emails Nimue Skin Technology SA. She is an ambassador for them and apologises that she won't be attending the announcement of a new jewellery line. This is a significant moment, because it indicates something unexpected has come up and she has to cancel at short notice.

7. So what's the big deal? What is so significant about **7 February** and **13 February**? According to Oscar's agent, Peet Van Zyl, these were extremely significant dates..

The reader is – at this point – perhaps rightfully scratching his or head, wondering: "Haven't we gone over this before?"

Yes we have. And I hinted – based on fairly limited data I had at the time – at what I thought was a *credible circumstantial scenario*.

But what happened in court today is, well, unprecedented. I'm not the only one who thinks so. On the Oscar Trial Television Channel Billy Gundelfinger, a famous South African lawyer said that "opening up character evidence in my view was a fatal mistake." Gundelfinger then made an uncharacteristic remark about guilt, and the channel suddenly jumped to a commercial break. When he was back on air, Gundelfinger explained his position. "You can also plead guilty," he said, "and enjoy a good result. A lesser sentence." He then implied a lot of negative character evidence is now in play, which will emerge through extensive cross-examination by Gerrie Nel.

"Nel in the normal course of the trial, and until now, the way wasn't open for him to do that."

Today's testimony in court and the disclosure of just a few details (which may seem incidental) has *significantly strengthened* this 'credible scenario' I've already put forward into something beyond mere credibility. I leave it to the reader (and perhaps the state prosecutor) to determine how 'high' this likelihood may be.

We will look at the details Van Zyl disclosed in court now and then get back to Capacity Relations. Then, all that remains is to fit the final pieces into the puzzle – which will get us finally to *Motive*.

The Agent's Two Key Revelations

Captain Spock [in Star Trek, the Undiscovered Country]: *Is it possible that we two, you and I, have grown so old and so inflexible that we have outlived our usefulness?*

In this section we deal with:

Two Revelations

Two Publications

Two Demonstrations

Two Obfuscations

Capacity Relations

Below I've highlighted a quartet of pertinent tweets that emerged from the proceedings on day 35 of the Oscar Pistorius murder trial (1 July 2014):

@GiaNicolaides #OscarPistorius has his hand over his face, as his manager talks about how he wanted Reeva to accompany him to sporting events in 2013. GN

@ewnreporter #OscarTrial Van Zyl: refers to correspondence between himself and a race organiser on 13/2. In it he asked for flight tickets for Reeva. BB

@GiaNicolaides · #OscarPistorius Van Zyl: Reeva was also going to join Oscar at a race in Brazil on 31 March.

@RobynCurnowCNN Peet van Zyl wearing a suit and tie, looks back and forth from Nel to Judge, as he faces Nel's barrage of questions about #oscarpistorius

And Nel summed up what the multitudes were thinking, including shivers of eavesdropping sharks:

"I never expected this to happen, today."

Peet Van Zyl began by defining his role as per IAAF definitions (ironically enough) and revealed he'd first met Oscar ten years ago (in 2004) and started a business relationship with Oscar in 2006. At that stage Oscar was around eighteen years old, and was working with Ray Wicksell (whom I've already mentioned).

Van Zyl then described the nature of his job, which he said was to secure competitions and races for his client, as well as to "negotiate and acquire brand ambassador agreements, sponsorships and endorsements."

Now that the reader is intimately familiar with the broader context, we can return to Barry Roux's seemingly innocent question:

"Did he involve her in his career?"

Now observe carefully how Peet Van Zyl responds. Instead of simply saying, "Yes," Van Zyl, at 11:01 tells us he had a meeting with his client (Oscar) as his home on 7 February 2013. The purpose of the meeting was to plan Oscar's year. Van Zyl said they laid a calendar out on Oscar's large dinner table, and put all the contracts alongside. Together they needed to identify their main target so they could plan Oscar's season. Unequivocally, Van Zyl reveals the whole year hinges around the (14th) IAAF World Championships in Moscow (from 10 - 18 August 2013).

Van Zyl says what they then do is work backwards from there, and develop a training plan.

Hold on. What was the question Barry Roux asked again? Did Oscar involve Reeva in his career? And instead of giving a straight answer, he reveals quite an intimate portrait of Oscar's strategic infrastructure. This already suggests that they were planning to integrate Reeva, somehow, into the innermost sanctums of Oscar's world. She would be involved, she would have a role somehow, in the overall Moneyspinning. That was part of the plan.

Easy now. A few hands are going into the air, and I know what you're thinking. But you the reader need to stick to the narrative. The question was:

"Did he involve her in his career?"

Not: Did he ask Reeva to come along as a travelling companion. Oscar and his agent saw her role as far more *strategic* than that. And that's not speculation.

Van Zyl reveals two particular events, a race in Brazil (against Oliveira) on March 31, and a second in Manchester on 25 May. Van Zyl said "Mr Pistorius specifically asked if Miss Steenkamp could accompany him on these two trips. He'd never asked me this before," Van Zyl admitted.

"Why do you want to do this?" he asked his client.

"I actually want Miss Steenkamp to see what my world is about...so she can understand why I can't go to events or functions with her...events I can't go to due to my own sponsor commitments..."

By using the word 'world' Oscar is talking his work. So Reeva would essentially accompany him to races, interviews and events. Oscar's world, Oscar's interviews, Oscar's events. And of course, Oscar's sponsors – not Reeva's.

The reader may be tempted to say: so what.

No. Not 'so what'. Because what Van Zyl reveals next is truly jaw-dropping. He provides evidence of an email he sent to Andy

Caine, the event director (or similar) of the Manchester City Games, on the evening of the 13th February. Possibly this guy:

http://uk.linkedin.com/pub/andy-caine/28/a55/635

Van Zyl is at pains to tell as *what time he sends the email.* 7:29 pm, on February 13th. At that time Oscar and Reeva, according to Oscar's version, were enjoying a happy dinner together. Oscar has never revealed what was discussed over dinner, or subsequent. In fact, what he has told us is that the two simply calmly, casually occupied the same space. One watched television while the other did Yoga. They did some unimportant web surfing at one point, including a session of car ogling.

Meanwhile, Oscar's agent was doing overtime trying to finalise the terms and conditions for Oscar to compete in the event. But...how was this relevant to Miss Steenkamp?

Van Zyl directs us to the 2nd page of his email.

"The following terms," he testified, "needed to be clarified." He required, he said, an additional business class ticket so that Reeva could accompany 'Mr Pistorius' on the same flight.

Van Zyl says there was already another contract in place, for an appearance in Brazil where Oscar and Oliveira would go, in Van Zyl's words, "head to head."

Van Zyl drops another bombshell right here. He tells us he'd also secured a place for 'Miss Steenkamp' to join Oscar on that trip.

Now what's interesting is the manner in which Van Zyl choreographs this disclosure. He doesn't give us the date or time of the correspondence regarding the trip to Brazil. Why not? Hopefully Nel will hammer on the specifics, because what's important to establish here is not Oscar's intentions (in this particular instance), or Oscar's willingness to include Reeva in his plans, but quite the opposite.

Those twitterstreams weren't put up (painstakingly, I might add) for nothing. What they reveal is, up to 13 February 2013, a sequestrated brand strategy. We will get to *who*, *why* and *what* were the reasons behind this at the end of this section. For the moment. The question we need to shine the spotlight on is:

Did Reeva want to be involved in her boo's career? It's clear Oscar wanted her, and I've speculated on this many times now, that he needed her to leverage his brand (as strange as that may seem, given her relatively weaker brand power).

Now, allow me to surgically remove a snippet from the social media correspondence in the preceding section. It may have seemed random and even messy, but it's really taking shape now. Look at this:

RS: **I'm always on your side and pro-you and your career, but mostly pro-us and the health of our relationship. We are important to me.**

OP: **That message meant a lot to me.**

But Oscar didn't quite get the message. Reeva isn't saying "Sign me up here" she's saying she's on his side, but the relationship is more important to her than his career. This is quite an incredible concession. Remember Reeva in January has revealed she is moving yet again, and is still not in tip top shape financially. Oscar is basically inviting her into his career, which would solve all her material concerns in a flash. From accommodation, to... Well, what would she, what could she get out of it besides exposure to the high life (which she already had). And what about her sponsors? What about her brands?

"Flight tickets for five. Mr. Pistorius, Ampie Louw (Oscar's coach), Van Zyl himself, a 'physio' and Miss Steenkamp."

The document, evidence of the flight confirmation probably, is submitted by Oscar's defence counsel as exhibit WWW.

Roux asks Van Zyl to describe the contents in further detail. Van Zyl says this is an email "between myself and the organiser in Brazil." It includes terms and agreements, and stipulated in the contract is that Miss Steenkamp would accompany Mr Pistorius to Brazil. While Van Zyl provides the time and date of the Manchester email, he fails to mention these in the second (which is actually the first email). Presumably these appear on the documents themselves.

What are the two crucial revelations?

> 1. On the night of **13 February** Oscar's agent was arranging air tickets with race organisers. This was in play while Reeva was at his house. Also in play, was Valentine's Day.

> 2. On **7 February**, Oscar informed his agent that he intended to include Reeva in his CAREER plans.

I've already alerted the reader to a potentially mischievous tactic, where Van Zyl first discloses the second trip (in May, to Manchester, and his arrangements made on February 13 and then subsequently discloses the first trip (at the end of March, to Brazil). But he doesn't tell us when this was arranged. Then he jumps back to that meeting on 7 February and reveals a discussion he had with Oscar surrounding a concert, in Tuscany, Italy.

"Why don't you impress her, take her to this..." Van Zyl suggested. Interestingly, Oscar's career plans seem not to include entertainment, but basically a tour of his 'world'. Van Zyl suggests to Oscar that Reeva, a classy girlfriend by any measure, would appreciate Andrea Bocelli in concert. There also seems to be a link between this suggestion and Brooklyn Travel in Pretoria.

How did his client respond to his innovative suggestions at romance? "He was excited."

Now Barry Roux asks Van Zyl:

"Did you discuss it with her?"

And now I want to alert the reader to potential mischief in the way both Roux and Van Zyl are disclosing this information. Because we don't get any information on whether Oscar discussed Brazil and Manchester with Reeva. If he did or didn't, if she accepted or didn't accept, we aren't explicitly told. It's implied, because "arrangements" are being made on her behalf, but let's also be clear on this – on 13 February, after 7pm.

What we are told, vividly, in no uncertain terms that Reeva was thrilled by this idea of being 'romanced'.

Van Zyl:"He phoned on his iPhone...it was a video call...[then] passed the phone on to me...[to] give her the good news...[I] informed her she was going to Brazil and Manchester."

We're told Reeva was very excited. "Very ecstatic to be travelling with us."

So...was she excited to be travelling to Bocelli? Probably. Was she also excited to be going to Brazil and Manchester? Maybe. It's implied. And at this point, it's actually not crucial whether she agreed to go to Brazil and Manchester or not. What's significant were these arrangements were made so close to the incident, including the night of the incident. What's also significant, in my view (and it is intuition, nothing more) is that if Reeva had agreed to go, why had her social media (Facebook and Twitter) not revealed these plans? Not even hinted at them. If she was to be part of Oscar's career:

"Did he involve her in his career?"

It's clear that she would have to indicate a willingness to put aside her career. Were there any signs of that between the 'excited' phone call on the 7th, and her death a week later?

Or...and here's a hint where this is going...were there other signs. Problems. *Hurdles*?

Now, two considerations:

> 1. **13 February: It's a difficult a thing... it's a sh***y thing** and you're a nice guy. I guess these things happen and **we can just hope they work out for the best**. You are... more than cared for. Your health and **future monetary blessings far outweigh this hurdle**. I can promise you that. This Whatsapp message is sent to Oscar on 13 February, around midday. At the same time she's gently suggesting that instead of her seeing him (she has a commitment that night anyway), he spends time with his family. She suggests Carl (his brother) and M (possibly a reference to Aimee, his sister). Does this sound like someone who has signed up for two or three exciting trips abroad? Or does it sound like there are difficulties, shitty things, things that happen, hurdles and 'hoping they work out for the best'.
>
> 2. **What happens to Reeva between January 31 and February 7**, the latter is the day Oscar and his agent decide to include Reeva in their career plans for Oscar? Well, rather a lot!

>January 31, 2013 via Instagram Time to get physical and burn some leftover Xmas ass before **my event later. #CosmoSexyMen**

>Via Facebook: February 4, 2013Hey everyone!!! Follow me on Twitter and Instagram @reevasteenkamp Have a blessed week!!!

>February 4, 2013 Grab a copy of the latest @People_SA I'm wearing a few numbers to inspire those ladies looking to spoil their men on Valentines Day #Love Charleen Ruthven **shared Ice Model Management Johannesburg's photo.**

>February 5, 2013REEVA / Current People Magazine

>7 Feb 2013 @reevasteenkamp · At the press launch of **@TropikaIOT5** OMG let's watch Episode 1 ..... *bites nails*

>7 Feb 2013 With my girl @pearlthusi at the **@tropikaiot5** launch this morning at the #MunroHotel http://instagr.am/p/Vbmo2cwPYf/

>7 Feb 2013 **When it takes you an entire day to try and compose a fitting response, a lacking one at that, rather leave it. It's just substandard.**

That last message may be directed at Oscar, who has perhaps not paid much heed to Reeva's career. "Oscar, did you know I'm going to be on Tropika Island Of Treasure?" "Oscar did you see me in X magazine?"

No. Because, as Nel might say, it's all about...?

Another important point is, based on Van Zyl, the 7th of February is the day they inform Reeva she has won a triple jackpot, to Brazil, Manchester (the UK) and Italy. She doesn't sound too excited on the 7th. Not a hint or a hair. Well, not about that anyway. But she is excited, very excited about her career. The 7th is a big day. There's a launch for her Tropika thing in the morning, and in the evening, the Virgin Active Awards (where both social media streams have zero endorsements of one another.) In the days prior to the 7th, Reeva is in People Magazine, and on that day and in the days thereafter, she is plugging "Tropika Islands of Treasure" again, and again, and again. What is her very last tweet on the 13th? Yes, it's about HER career. She cares very much about her career. Look!

What happens after February 7?

[Retweeteed] @Zalebs · 8 Feb 2013 **Tropika Island of Treasure** season 5 is about to hit a TV screen near you! Are you a fan of the show? http://bit.ly/YYuGnh

@reevasteenkamp · 8 Feb 2013 Before you lift a pen or raise your voice to criticise, acknowledge people's circumstances. You don't know their struggles. Their journey.

@reevasteenkamp · 8 Feb 2013 Lying on a blanky in the garden with my @gi_myers breathing in some fresh air and chatting about life.

@TheLinkTVShow · 13 Feb 2013 Tune into @TheLinkTVShow right now 4 a sneak peek of "**Tropika Islands of Treasure**" @reevasteenkamp, @akaworldwide, @PearlThusi #tiot5

Reeva cares about Oscar too, but not at the expense of *her* career. I've said it before, if he's a determined athlete, she's also an independent, determined, passionate woman. And she's probably a lot more mature and emotionally independent than her boo. I mean, consider that she isn't asking for Oscar's help to boost her brand, quite the opposite. She is asking for his help in terms of the admin side, helping her with the fine print to her contracts, but she still wants to run her own show, and she still intends to remain the star if her show.

Oscar's three invitations to these three exotic destinations are not small, short, once off trips. It is a long term investment, and it is essentially a request that Reeva either put her career on hold, or simply abandons it altogether.

But Reeva's rebuff to Oscar's 'career' advances shouldn't be in the least surprising. Remember what she told Heat magazine?

"We haven't been talking to the media because I don't want to get it tainted," Reeva told the magazine.

"<u>I don't want anything coming in the way of his career</u>. He's such an amazing athlete."

"<u>I'm trying to work on my modelling career</u> and remove myself from the whole FHM stigma," she said. "<u>I want to be seen as a classic model</u>."

Andre Neveling, heat South Africa editor, said: "... as a couple they agreed to do an exclusive cover shoot with heat in April."

April? It was February 7. Why April? April was giving them another month together essentially.

Neveling: <u>it took a lot of convincing to get the couple to agree to a sit-down interview</u>. They were discussing the idea on the red carpet of the Sports Industry Awards.

> "They spoke openly about everything," he said. "It started in October [?] and they began dating in November and <u>they asked to hold off on the cover story until April to give them some time</u>. That said to me that they were serious."

http://www.citypress.co.za/news/reeva-feared-lies-could-ruin-relationship-with-oscar/

That says to me they also had some important issues to iron out. Such as how do we keep both our careers rolling? And how do you maintain a relationship when you're overseas for six months at a time? Well, Reeva had experienced this – with Warren – and her Facebook timeline shows it was a painful period of protracted absences. Her social media is also replete with a sense of 'learning life lessons'. Was she going to repeat the same 'mistakes' with Oscar? Long distance relationships. Infrequent (exhausting) trips abroad?

And one has to wonder, who needed convincing to sit down as a couple? Who asked to hold off the story? Wasn't it Reeva? She wanted to preserve her career – first and foremost – and if possible, preserve her career with Oscar. Of course, if he was leaving in March 31 for Brazil (without her) she'd be in a better position to gauge the long term potential of the relationship...when? Yes, in April. That would be when Reeva would make her call.

But what was going on in Oscar's world?

As it turns out, some pretty momentous stuff.

Barry Roux: "What was the position regarding Mr Pistorius' financial future in February 2013?

Peet Van Zyl: "Due to amazing performances in London at the Olympic games and Paralympics

His profile had been raised to that of a global icon."

Van Zyl said that in the end the London Games were about two athletes, Oscar and Usain Bolt. And, he declared, "The media will agree with me."

Following the Oscar's triumphs in 2012, the marketing marvel found himself, Van Zyl adds, "in a business world with lots of opportunities. Corporate companies wanted to be associated with Oscar."

Van Zyl says they saw synergy potential between their brands and Oscar's, synergy between his (Oscar's) values and their values. He added that these companies wanted to include Oscar in their marketing campaigns. Van Zyl added that Oscar's net worth before the Games had increased by a factor of "five or six" by 2013.

During their meeting on 7 February they discussed contracts worth millions, contracts that would see the disabled athlete through till 2017 (a year after Rio).

In 2017, Van Zyl pointed out, "[Oscar] would have announced his retirement."

On the 7th of February they were looking at their current sponsors, and Oscar's brand ambassadorial roles up to his retirement and post retirement. That's pretty extensive, long term planning. The contracts also entailed "share options, merchandising" etc.

Van Zyl also described his client as "Very aware of [business opportunities] and [a] very astute businessman.

"He was very aware of his role and the financial implications he stood to gain." And lose.

Two Publications

Though evidently unprepared, Nel cleverly began his cross-examination by concentrating first on two seemingly innocuous topics. Firstly, Oscar's predisposition to speeding. And secondly, on the question of anger, an incident 'with another athlete', where the athlete 'asked to be moved to another room. This narrative has dealt in some detail with the later. Having riled up Van Zyl suffiently, Nel then went for the jugular and asked Van Zyl, point blank:

"Did you discuss the incident with Mr Pistorius?"

We'll get to that.

First let's examine two slip ups by Van Zyl.

Two Demonstrations, Two Obfuscations

1. Speeding – was Van Zyl aware of reports that Oscar was in the habit of driving {recklessly] fast?

2. Anger – was Van Zyl aware of an additional incident, where Oscar's anger seemed to propel a roommate (in the Olympic village) into alternative living quarters, because Oscar was constantly arguing/screaming on the phone?

Van Zyl claimed to be pretty ignorant on both counts. Then Nel referenced an article by a 'British journalist', who he said came to Oscar's home, stayed with him and saw the gun in his bedroom. At this point I thought Nel was referring to the Sokolove article, published in the New York Times.

Here it is again:

http://www.nytimes.com/2012/01/22/magazine/oscar-pistorius.html?pagewanted=all&_r=0

And here's the relevant extract:

The first time I drove with him, I peeked at the speedometer and saw the needle on 250 kilometres per hour. (That's 155 miles per hour.) People congregate around his vehicle — the "white monster," his manager [Van Zyl] *called it — just to hear it idle.*

Wow – 250km/h isn't fast it's 'are you insane'. At more than double the maximum speed limit, it's also illegal. And how reckless is it for a legless man to be driving at these speeds? A man with no feet? But what about temperament? Because that's what we're fishing at now, isn't it. Character.

Pistorius is, as well, blessed with an uncommon temperament — a fierce, even frenzied need to take on the world at maximum speed and with minimum caution. It is an athlete's disposition, that of a person who believes himself to be royalty of a certain kind — a prince of the physical world.

Hanging out with Pistorius can be a great deal of fun. You also quickly understand that he is more than a little crazy. I asked him about the tattoo on his left ... "I went into an all-night tattoo parlor," he said. "Some Puerto Rican guy did it. It took from 2 a.m. to about 8:30. I think he was falling asleep after a while, which is why it's a little squiggly at the bottom. But I like it that way. To me, it makes it look more authentic."

In 2008, Pistorius crashed his boat-

[Actually it was February 2009:

http://mg.co.za/article/2009-02-24-pistorius-boating-accident-what-actually-happened]

-into a submerged pier on a river south of Johannesburg. His face and body hit the steering wheel, and he broke two ribs, his jaw and an eye socket. Doctors had to sew 172 stitches in his face....

Sokolove next references a nasty fall on a dirt bike.

The people around Pistorius, Sokolove writes, *worry about his risk-taking, but there's only so much they can do. His manager, Peet van Zyl, shrugged when I asked him about it. "It's the nature of the man," he said. "At least we did get the motorbike away from him."*

Beyond his physical disability, Pistorius is unlike his peers in another, less visible way. Lots of athletes at his level hoard their energy for a single purpose...Pistorius's mind and body do not easily come to rest...The competition season, which takes place mainly in Europe and stretches through the spring and summer, can be difficult for him. "When we're on the circuit, you wake up, you eat, you stretch," he said. "You go back to your room and watch a TV series or try to take a nap. You have lunch, go for another stretch or an ice bath and go back to your room. It can be very boring. I've spent like six hours on the Internet, just Googling, or watching stupid YouTube videos."

Fair enough. A few observations, but nothing controversial, nothing cutting to the bone, as it were. But then there's this:

The Cheetah blades are meant for running and no other purpose. The first thing you notice when Pistorius wears them is that his balance is not good; he sways when he tries to stand still and looks for a place to sit down, like someone on ice skates who has just exited the rink. A running track is an oval — it's not hard to understand why Pistorius has an easier time on the straightaways than the turns.

...I asked [his coach, Ampie Louw] *why he thought Pistorius was so fast. "He can move his legs fast. If you can do that, you can run fast..."*

Pistorius is nearing the start of his competitive season, which begins in February. His mission is clear: Run faster than the Olympic "A" qualifying time of 45.30 in the 400 meters, and at the same time be one of the three fastest South Africans in order to earn a guaranteed spot in London.

The scientific and cultural questions involving Pistorius are not easily answered. One way to make sport seem fair is for all competitors to be alike, which surely disqualifies him. Another is to keep "enhancements" from infiltrating the sanctity of sport. ...

Pistorius refers to himself as "a sportsman." As we sat one afternoon in his living room, he talked about the inquiry into his eligibility in terms of a specific kind of self-discovery: is his presence on the track fair to competitors? "The purpose for me wasn't to be able to say to everybody, 'Look, I don't have an advantage,' " he said. "I really wanted to find out, 'Do I have an advantage?' Because I don't want to be competing in a sport where I feel that I'm here not on my talent and my hard work but because of a piece of equipment."

Pistorius stresses that he is proud to compete in Paralympic competitions. But he believes the strongest argument for his participation in able-bodied events is <u>his vast superiority over disabled athletes</u> who run on the same Cheetah prosthetic legs in the 400 meters...It's not like at this level I can go out and run a low 44, just because I said this is the day I want to do that. That's never going to happen."

Which is probably true. But also surprising to hear from someone of Pistorius's hellbent temperament. I wondered if there might be an element of self-protection in his thinking. If he meets his stated goal, he would continue to be well compensated, well liked and respected. His good life would get only better. If he could somehow pull off a miracle and make it to the medal stand, there might be no end of controversy.

An article that questions –invalidates, interrogates – Oscar's *raison d'être* is very damaging indeed. It's damaging to his brand, to his ability to perform at all. It undermines his entire career.

Sokolove also briefly mentions Oscar's 'irritability' and his 'insomnia', and walks us through a day in the life (and the house) where Reeva lost her life, as well as a night in the life of a (restless) gun enthusiast.

Pistorius lives in the house with a friend from high school, an engineer who moonlights as a mixed-martial-arts fighter. Pistorius had recently broken off a relationship with his longtime girlfriend, though another young woman was visiting when we got there. As he put together lunch for all of us — fruit smoothies, breaded chicken fillets he pulled from the refrigerator — he mentioned that a security alarm in the house had gone off the previous night, and he had grabbed his gun and tiptoed downstairs. (It turned out to be nothing.)

I asked what kind of gun he owned, which he seemed to take as an indication of my broader interest in firearms. I had to tell him I didn't own any. "But you've shot one, right?" Actually, I hadn't. Suddenly, I felt like one of those characters in a movie who must be schooled on how to be more manly.

"We should go to the range," he said. He fetched his 9-millimeter handgun and two boxes of ammunition. We got back in the car and

drove to a nearby firing range, where he instructed me on proper technique. Pistorius was a good coach. A couple of my shots got close to the bull's-eye, which delighted him. "Maybe you should do this more," he said. "If you practiced, I think you could be pretty deadly." I asked him how often he came to the range. "Just sometimes when I can't sleep," he said.

But Sokolove is more than likely not the British journalist Nel is referring to. Could it be this article by the Daily Mail's Jonathan McEvoy? The problem is this piece doesn't refer to speeding anywhere, or anger management issues. High irritation levels, on the other hand, can't be discounted.

http://www.iol.co.za/sport/athletics/i-m-done-talking-about-my-legs-oscar-1.1121468

Even so, here's where Van Zyl's testimony, to my mind, unravels. Nel has already established that an agent's role is to manage positive and negative publicity surrounding an athlete. Nel asks Van Zyl if he considered the basic narrative of Sokolove's/McEvoy's article 'negative'?

Van Zyl: "I did read an article about that...I remember recalling reading that."

What? You 'remember recalling'?

Nel: "Would you say it was a positive or negative article?"

Van Zyl: "At that stage I didn't see anything negative..."

Van Zyl essentially seemed to making the case that he didn't always know what his client was doing, and it wasn't his business to know.

Did Oscar ever have arguments with Reeva?

"I wasn't aware of any arguments. For me," Van Zyl said, "it was really a case of him wanting to show Ms Steenkamp what his world as a professional athlete was about. You **have to be very strict** and professional if you want to achieve these goals that you've set yourself."

Yes, you do have to be strict:

- Strict about guns
- Strict about not sleeping
- Strict about dangerous driving
- Strict about tantrums (especially in public)
- Strict about the (non-athlete) friends you hand around with
- Strict about one's emotional state

Oscar, bitterly disappointed his girlfriend Samantha Taylor (his 'little Butterfly' and the 'one') wasn't joining him in London – he told her he didn't feel like going if she wasn't coming with. That's one dedicated Olympian! If he did, can you imagine Peet Van Zyl's face:

"Hi Peet, I've decided I'm not going."

"Why? Are you sick? What happened? Are you injured?"

"No, my girlfriend's not keen."

"What?"

"Ja Sam's not into it, so I think I'm also gonna give it a miss. But thanks for setting everything up. Maybe things will work out in Rio. Chat to you later."

Do not be deceived! The life of a professional athlete and a sports agent is tough. It's a hard grind. Van Zyl's right, if you want to do it properly, if you're a professional, you have to apply discipline. You've got to be strict. But how strict was Van Zyl on his clients nocturnal habits?

Apparently, not very.

Even though Oscar said he took a loaded weapon *everywhere* he went (after the incident Oscar declared himself cured of his gun worship), but this fact of Oscar's life seems to have escaped Van Zyl's notice. If Van Zyl was wise to Oscar's gun toting as late as November 2012, it means for the *entire* eight year period that he has mentored (or not?) his client, it somehow escaped his notice.

Was he unaware that Oscar had trouble sleeping? And what he did when he couldn't sleep? And how likely is it that the man in charge of Oscar's business interests didn't read every single word (including words about him) published in the prestigious New York Times.

According to Van Zyl he noticed Oscar carrying a gun for the first time in November 2012.

Van Zyl: "I asked why Mr Pistorius had gun. He specifically replied to me he was carrying a gun because he was fearing for his own safety."

If Oscar feared for his safety, what did Van Zyl do about it? Recommend counselling, sharpening security, a bodyguard?

Van Zyl also didn't provide very convincing testimony on Oscar's roaming roommate at London Olympics.

He didn't even seem to know who it was or what happened. He didn't seem to know why the roommate had suffered itchy feet (or in Fourie's case, foot). An incident like this, at conceivably the most critical time in Oscar's career, and Van Zyl's unaware of the 'specifics'?

"What Oscar Pistorius did in his private life I wasn't always aware of."

Not?

"Mr Pistorius didn't discuss the relationship with me" (yet Oscar asks Van Zyl if Reeva can join him on a business trip).

But why wouldn't Oscar discuss the roommate scenario? It could have major repercussions. It could damage his brand. At the very least, they could ascertain what – if any – damage had been done by that point. Was it in the press? Was it still coming out? Was the roommate bitter?

But Van Zyl is very disassociated. Very distant.

"We were made aware of that by SA Team Management."

'I don't even know who this specific athlete was...?"

Hang on, really?

Nel tells Van Zyl: "You're trying to avoid questions. Why did he want to leave the room?"

"He wanted to leave the room because..."

Behind Gerrie Nel, Oscar passes a note to his defence team.

"Is it difficult to say state negative things about Mr Pistorius?" Nel asks.

"It was dealt with within the team environment."

But you're his agent. What about his sponsors? Weren't they concerned?

"Why," Nel insists, "did the athlete not want to stay with the accused?"

"No I never discussed it because I never deemed it to be that important. Ampie Lous [Oscar's Coach] said 'Listen, we have moved Oscar to a different room. I was never informed that there were specifics."

Oscar's agent looked visibly irritated at this point. He was staring at Nel with his mouth ajar.

At this point Nel warned him: "Mr Van Zyl I'm not going to go away."

"Had you heard about it or read about it. Not if you were specifically told. Have you heard it, or read it?"

Long pause.

The testimony appeared to strain Oscar as well. He started wiping his face with his hands. But the door was already open. Nel could point and poke and question every controversial flare-up reported in local and international media.

James Grant, a legal expert, speaking on the Oscar Trial television channel explained what was happening during a brief adjournment. "This is character evidence. And character evidence," he said, "has already been opened by Oscar himself. What a good person, a good Christian he is. He's opened himself to be tested on that. That's how," Grant emphasised, "you open yourself to character evidence." Grant added that Nel could now cross examine Van Zyl on Oscar's bad character.

"Nel can call other witnesses to testify on bad character. I would absolutely do that. The door is wide open…"

"If you had one more person to call who would you call?" the host asked.

"A psychologist," Grant answered.

Interestingly, Arnu Fourie released this statement, perhaps an attempt to avoid implicating Oscar, overnight:

http://www.enca.com/fourie-clears-air-about-sharing-room-pistorius

Note that Fourie does not deny [the angry phone calls], he simply offers an alternative explanation for moving out.

Van Zyl appeared to playing semantics. He referenced two anger episodes, one related to media at an arrivals hall in Barcelona who 'stuffed a camera' in his – and Oscar's faces. Oscar was accused by this crew of cheating (in his continued insistence to run with able-bodied athletes). Van Zyl declared the science 'settled' on this matter, and hence, these 'abusive' question which they had to 'suffer' were completely out of line.

Interestingly the other incident that made the pair lose their tempers was at the BBC, on exactly the same question. Nel then asked if there wasn't a third incident. He had to remind Van Zyl of Oscar's outburst to Oliveira, where he accused Oliveira of cheating. Van Zyl said he wasn't there, so hadn't thought to mention it. No, on the anger incidents he was only referring to incidents he experienced firsthand. Nel then pertinently said:

"He called the person who beat him a cheat...you forgot about that."

More dissemination, obfuscation.

"But you know about it," Nel persisted. "You didn't tell the court about it."

"I only explained the specific instance when I was present."

"Did you deal with it?"

Van Zyl obfuscates.

"Please Mr Van Zyl, did you deal with it?"

Van Zyl gives a long answer with a lot of information.

Finally he admits, it was the "wrong place and time to react in this way." He then talks about one leg amputees who wanted the rules that applied to double amputees to be clarified (which would have been in his favour.) Interestingly, this appeal for clarification didn't come from other double amputees (in other words, athletes like Oscar).

Van Zyl goes on to say Oscar may drive fast, but he isn't reckless. 250km/h isn't reckless?

Nel asks him whether he read reports about Oscar driving recklessly.

"You never read...anything."

"I never read all those reports..."

Not even the one in the New York Times, quoting Van Zyl's comment of his car?

It doesn't take a wordsmith to appreciate how critical and damaging McEvoy's assessment of Oscar was. In fact, even I was surprised just how many potshots McEvoy takes at Oscar.

Mr Pistorius' love for guns – do you know about that?

As amiable and intelligent a sportsman as you would travel this far to meet, he is passionate, frustrated, angry at times, as he puts forward his case. "I think this will be one of the last interviews – maybe the last – I will ever do addressing this subject [competing against able-bodied athletes]," he says. "I'm pretty much done with it."

The debate then largely fell into abeyance. Until last month, that is, when Pistorius ran 45.07sec in Italy [Lignano] to qualify for the

World Championships. The fundamental questions were suddenly asked again.

The answers, he knows, must be more than simply emotional. It is not enough to admire his disability-defying spirit.... so forget the science.

What does his disability defying narrative?

McEvoy gives us his definition:

– screaming with joy as he threw himself and his toy motorbike down the stairs of the family house as a two-year-old, learning to wrestle at six, driving the car around the grounds of his home at nine, playing football, cricket, water polo and rugby at school, taking up running at 16 after smashing his knee on the rugby field, racing superbikes with a speed freak's relish (a fix he is rationing for now, even if he drives his BMW more like Lewis Hamilton) – and say he's inspirational,

No, the argument is taking place at the very fringes of scientific knowledge. Let's hear the case for the prosecution first. It is led by Dr Ross Tucker, a senior lecturer at the University of Cape Town's exercise science and sports medicine department.

"This is more like Formula One than athletics," he said. "Engineers can tinker with equipment to gain a speed advantage. Is that what we want? I think Pistorius does get an enormous advantage. Peter Weyand, one of the scientists who did the testing to clear him, recently published a paper saying he has a 12-second advantage. He should not have committed a number – that was a mistake – but the way he did it is sound, and when you look at the data, it's quite clear that Pistorius's mechanics are off the biological charts. So, too, are his metabolic markers.

Wow. This is Oscar's favourite worst topic. The able-bodied debate is what they have both characteristically lost their tempers about. Why? Because if the scientific argument is validated, it could extinguish Oscar's career overnight, and for that matter, Peet van Zyl's.

McEvoy quotes Oscar's nemesis here, Tucker: *"Pistorius 'stole' science to win that verdict [at the Court of SArbitration]. To hear Pistorius speak now, he's saying that 'the science cleared me'. It was the legal team and some, quite frankly, dishonest science that cleared him."*

If their narrative is based on dishonest science, how honest are the athlete and his agent? I mean, they're regularly confronted with this question of fairness? And how and where was Reeva supposed to fit into it? Or was she meant to be a distraction. Another attempt to control the narrative by dodging around it?

For my part, I am impressed to find McEvoy managed to extract what one may have suspected all along. That Oscar considers his detractors, principally the likes of Dr Ross Tucker, personal enemies. Let's have a look at a last extract from McEvoy's article (titled: I'M DONE TALKING ABOUT MY LEGS – OSCAR):

I mention Tucker's name to Pistorius. "I don't want to speak about him," he says, exasperated. The Pistorius camp is aware that Tucker is contacting the media to push his agenda. They say he has conducted no pertinent research. Nor, they say, has he published his views in a scientific journal, where it would be peer reviewed.

Pistorius adds: "There are many ill-informed arguments. There are people who are commenting for personal gain or to make a name for themselves or to be controversial.

"I know my opinion is right because I have sat with some of the top guys in the world. Hugh Herr has been voted by Time magazine as one of the smartest minds over the last decade. He really is a genius. Two others I have sat with are Robert Gailey and Rodger Kram. They have studied biomechanics and kinetics more than any other guys in the world.

"Hugh gets kind of worked up because a guy (Tucker, presumably) who has a background in sports science will come in and say his findings are wrong. It's like taking two racing drivers – one is a kart racer; the other is an F1 racer. They are both racing

drivers. But there is only one guy with the real knowledge and his views count more."

The IAAF now back Pistorius' stance, accepting the Court of Arbitration's decision without rancour.

Pistorius adds: "I didn't want to run if I was a cheat. I didn't want to have the slightest doubts in my mind.

"I believe in the purity of sport. I don't like people who take short cuts. I'd never be involved in sport if I had the slightest doubts.

"It does get to me quite hard. The worst thing is when somebody says my improvements this year are down to changing my prosthetic legs. My prosthetic legs have stayed the same for seven years, down to the bolts and the lining.

"Then I read somewhere that my legs travel faster than those of an able- bodied sprinter. In sprinting, your opposite arm and opposite leg travel together, so that would mean I am having to move my arms faster, which means I am having to burn more energy in my upper body."

McEvoy then plays Devil's Advocate.

Why, then, the doubters?

"This story, if you will forgive the expression, has legs," adds Herr. "There are people in the world, scientists and non-scientists, who are troubled by the idea of someone with an unusual body running against someone with a 'normal' body.

"People have said it will disrupt the sanctity of sport, the same language once used against those with dark-coloured skin. There remains a social, prejudicial perspective."

Back over his coffee, Pistorius gets out his mobile phone. Twitter is full of support. Words like 'inspiration' abound. He appreciates the sentiment but does not seek special adulation.

"They ask how I stay so positive," he says of some tweeters. "It's as if I wake up with a giant smile on my face each day. I have the same bad days as every athlete. Times when I get fed up with eating chicken for the 20th time that month. Or my body hurts. Small messages of support can lift you. In South Korea the media are apparently so excited by my being there.

"I am really blessed."

Where will it end? Will he go so fast that he wins, makes a final, or takes a medal? If so, the debate over the legality of his Cheetahs will rage on ever more intensely.

"I really do think it will be tough for me to get down to a mid-44," says Pistorius, whose personal best of 45.07sec is 0.46 off the fastest time this year, run by Grenadian Kirani James. "As for low 44s or 43s, I believe without being negative or cynical that's not a league I'm in.

"If I break 45 next year, even if it's 44.9, I'll be happy. When I ran my personal best last month, it was the only perfect race I have ever done in seven or eight years of running. My back was sore. My neck was sore. I couldn't train for a week. I struggled to sleep for two days.

"All I want is not to spend my career discussing my legs. I've trained as much as anyone. I have sacrificed as much as anyone.

"It's like you interviewing an able-bodied sprinter and asking him if his pair of shoes make him great. He spends half his life saying, "It's not my shoes; it's my training".

"I'm training s*** hard. And if my shoes are so great, why are other Paralympians not running the times I am?"

It sounded, to a compelling degree, as if he had answered his own question.

Why am I the fastest? Because my shoes are so great. And Oscar Pistorius often compares his legs to shoes. His interview on Larry King Now is one case in point. But is this the inference McEvoy is making? That it is, in the final analysis, all about the legs? And his title draws special attention to this. Can Van Zyl really call this critique positive?

And was he really unaware of Oscar's fiery temper? He describes his own temper as worse than Oscar's, if true, hardly a feather in either of their caps. Especially given the following:

http://www.theaustralian.com.au/news/world/oscar-pistorius-charming-but-with-a-fiery-temper/story-fnb64oi6-1226578627685?nk=5f659dee2c4d36ae43e288c8a478edf3

And here's the relevant extract:

...his temper has flared in private. Soon after Pistorius returned to South Africa from London last year, he allegedly threatened to break the legs of Quinton van der Burgh, a millionaire television producer.

According to reports, Pistorius accused the businessman of an alleged infidelity with a girlfriend during the London Olympics. Marc Batchelor, a former footballer and a friend of Mr van der Burgh, intervened and Pistorius issued an indirect threat of violence through him, it was claimed. "This is not something I want to talk about," Pistorius said at the time.

Mr van der Burgh stressed that the unnamed woman in question was not Pistorius's girlfriend, and declined to comment further. Police were involved but no arrests or charges were brought.

In 2009, Pistorius was arrested for assault after slamming a door on a woman and spent a night in police custody. Family and friends said it was an accident and charges were dropped.

In his autobiography Pistorius spoke at length of the "fiery relationship" he had with Ms Miles. Rows were regular and "nasty", though there was no mention of physical violence. After one argument, Mr Pistorius attempted to drive 650km from Durban to Johannesburg to see her at 3am, but had a serious crash on the way.

It resembles what Jani Allan so aptly described in her 'Letter to Oscar' as a "wasteland of privilege and recidivism," doesn't it?

Capacity Relations

There are three possibilities why Reeva wasn't going to play second fiddle to Oscar's career.

1. It was her personal choice.

2. Capacity Relations made a recommendation, which Reeva agreed with (or went along with) believing it was in her interests.

3. Capacity Relations wished to hold onto their client, especially one with a brand –linked to one of the world's most powerful brand ambassadors – about to 'explode', which would have been good for Capacity Relations, as long as they could maintain contractual control over their client.

There is an Afrikaans saying 'die vark in die verhaal'. It literally translates to 'the pig in the story'. It's possible (though personally I'm not convinced) that Reeva was keen to join Oscar on his adventure. She certainly appeared to have genuine feelings of affection, and even love, for Oscar, especially in the beginning. And her 'career' was still very young and uninformed at that stage. And let's face it, at 29, 30, Reeva was not. Her best years – certainly in modelling – were almost behind her. Oscar could be just the ticket at just the right time. But Capacity Relations didn't think so. And it appears that, certainly from Oscar's intentions for Reeva, and specifically how she could enhance his brand and enhance his career, Capacity Relations threw a spanner in the works. They told her, insisted, that Oscar was bad for her brand. And she listened.

Perhaps they had good reason. But at the end of the day, consider this. Reeva had 3000 followers on Twitter and even fewer on Facebook. Oscar's numbers were closer to 350 000. Was it really such good PR, good tactical advice to play down their relationship? Even on social media? Why?

It may or may not be relevant (probably not) but the owner of Capacity Relations is Sarit Tomlinson. There is another Tomlinson – a Simon Tomlinson – who is from Johannesburg, and a Managing Director at WorldsView Sports. Perhaps the Tomlinson's wanted Reeva and Oscar with them? Or, perhaps not.

But it is certainly possible, in the greater scheme of things, that Oscar could have been of tremendous strategic benefit to Reeva's brand (giving herself enormous clout, TV time, and opportunities, much as David Beckham's bigger, better brand leveraged Victoria's). A football player and a famous singer who can't really sing – one could do worse. A disabled athlete, an icon, and an attractive model and paralegal – yes, one could do worse.

Ultimately, Oscar probably needed Reeva (or felt he needed her) more than she needed him. She may have needed him financially but was not that sort of person.

And then consider the ethical dilemma. Reeva was an intelligent, principled person. She had studied law after all, and cared about abuse, to women, children and animals. On the morning of her death she had prepared a speech. It was about sticking to one's guns. Not being bullied. And being brave and making your voice heard. Reeva was all about equity. Fairness. Fair play. If she did not see through Oscar's narrative in January or February, she probably would have eventually. She may have suspected – as early as February – that while she loved him, her hero was a gleaming fake.

If she didn't, he showed her, in the early hours of February 14.

Motive – the undiscovered country

"To be, or not to be, that is the question—
Whether 'tis Nobler in the mind to suffer
The Slings and Arrows of outrageous Fortune,
Or to take Arms against a Sea of troubles,
And by opposing end them? To die, to sleep—
No more; and by a sleep, to say we end
The Heart-ache, and the thousand Natural shocks
That Flesh is heir to? 'Tis a consummation
Devoutly to be wished. To die, to sleep,
To sleep, perchance to Dream; Aye, there's the rub,
For in that sleep of death, what dreams may come,
When we have shuffled off this mortal coil,
Must give us pause. There's the respect
That makes Calamity of so long life:
For who would bear the Whips and Scorns of time,
The Oppressor's wrong, the proud man's Contumely,
The pangs of despised Love, the Law's delay – Hamlet, William Shakespeare

Now we deal with motive. The reader should note that amygdala flooding (or hijacking) can be triggered by fear. Or rage. For most of his life, Oscar has internalised the idea that he is just as good, if not better than able-bodied people. He is constantly competing – and thus comparing himself – and thus VALIDATING himself against the realm of the able-bodied. And Oscar has done exceptionally well at projecting this image – which is no more than a persona – of a disabled man who has, for all intents and purposes, overcome his disability.

But there is a difference between the appearance of things, and reality, as we have seen, and as we shall see.

What we fail to appreciate is that Oscar's internalised idea of competing, and fighting to compete in the world of able-bodied athletics, was playing out equally off the athletics track. Because it was unseen, undisclosed, it is easy for us to assume that Oscar's disability (within pedestrian society) wasn't an issue to him. It wasn't something that concerned him, it wasn't something he worried about.

Except, we know it was.

Van Zyl referenced a specific incident on a plane. Oscar, he said, was in the habit of wearing his prostheses throughout these long flights. But on this occasion Oscar removed his prostheses because of severe blisters on his stumps. He had his legs covered by a blanket so no one could see his disability. We know that Oscar was in the habit of covering his prosthesis even at home, usually throwing a towel or a t-shirt over them, to conceal them from view.

"At some stage one of the legs fell over and when an air hostess tried to pick it up politely, Oscar Pistorius had felt someone close and (he) was startled," Van Zyl said.

He was startled. **

"He grabbed his leg from her."

It sounds like Oscar was sleeping, and when he woke up, he was shocked to discover an air hostess holding his leg. Van Zyl says even though the air hostess was trying to help Oscar – out of politeness – he grabbed his leg. It's possible if Oscar was sleeping that Van Zyl was also sleeping, perhaps the entire cabin was sleeping, hence the air hostess was the only one who saw the leg in the aisle, and offered to return it to him. His response was such to apparently alert and disturb Van Zyl. And despite the air hostesses politeness, Van Zyl, who is always in Oscar's corner, concedes Oscar 'grabbed' it from her. A lapse, certainly from Oscar's usual courtesy with strangers.

The price for Oscar in maintaining his vigil, to consistently project a persona, of presenting himself as able-bodied (despite fatigue, discomfort and physical pain) meant Oscar could not simultaneously admit his vulnerabilities. He could not admit his weaknesses. He could not share his fears and anxieties and the terrible loneliness that accompanies such a journey. A big gap, therefore forms between the outward persona, and the inward persona. And the greater the outward persona, the more critical the desire to conceal those inward insecurities. Especially when contracts, endorsements and one's career depended on that bravado, on keeping up these appearances, on maintaining a brave face.

But whether we like it or not, these deceptions exact a toll on us. The human consciousness continually seeks to establish congruence between the world within and the world without. This was Oscar's true journey, and his true heroism lay in his ability to take the problem of his own life, and address it with his physical Life Force. But more than that. The deep desire to appear able-bodied (normal), to achieve parity with the world extended into his ordinary relationships with people. And especially his relationships with women. Here he was called to make himself available emotionally and physically, and be himself. Not conceal himself, reveal himself. And what if, when he did, the person who he needed in so many ways, not just for love, companionship but also for validation – what if when he reached out to that special trusted person, she rejected him. That rejection:

- Negative response

- refusal

- Denial
- Rebuff
- Denunciation
- Refutation
- Dismissal
- Elimination
- Invalidation

To Oscar, to his mind and being, the rejection becomes the elimination of *who he is*. The denuniciation of his persona, the Invalidation of his journey. The loss of all he has devoted so much, his entire life, his being, to building. But we know on every occasion that journalists have called into question the validity of this journey (into the arena of able-bodied athletics) Oscar and Van Zyl have lost it.

We are finally at the heart of it all.

The key to motive lies either in fear, or rage. Which was it? Because on 14 February 2013, sometime after 03:10am, *something happened* to Oscar. Something that involved certainly *a degree* of automatism. It is this writer's belief that two major forces converged in Oscar's psyche. At the critical moment, not one but *two* narratives crucial to Oscar's identity came decisively under threat.

I felt trapped.

There was no time to think.

I did not fire at Reeva! [he breaks down, wails, he's in tears.]

Remember?

Watch it again:

https://www.youtube.com/watch?v=3vl_AcMIt8o

More details here: http://www.dailymail.co.uk/news/article-2604108/We-love-Fans-greet-Oscar-Pistorius-hugs-music-white-balloons-arrives-court-second-week-box.html

On 11 February Oscar tweeted that it was a month to his first race. His season was starting. On 13 February, he'd make arrangements and finalise things so Reeva could join him. It would be his best year yet! But then something happened, something Oscar could never have imagined. Reeva didn't want to be part of his career. She had her own, and ny February 2013, it was hot, scorching.. Reeva's refusal to join Oscar on two legs of his athletic journey in 2013 (Brazil and Manchester) would have been painful enough. It would be many lonely months on the road for him. Months of hotels and exotic places, months of putting up a brave face to the press, months of bravado and beating back the cynics.

He may have understood in some small sense, yes, Reeva had her own career going on. Perhaps, at the very least she could join him for that Bocelli concert. "You're still coming to that, aren't you? At least give me that!" It may have been still early in the night when they negotiated one concession, only to grasp there were more obstacles, major obstacles standing in their way. Her career was a drop to his ocean, but on some level, he could accept it. Maybe they could find a way. Maybe she would work something out. He could go along with that, he could do all that, but having no one to comfort him, no one to share in his adventure wasn't going to be fun.

That was only the first narrative. The athlete's journey. He would have to continue on that lonely road without her. It was heartbreaking that she wouldn't, or couldn't accompany him, just as it had been devastating to him when Samantha Taylor hadn't joined him in London.

But far more excruciating would be her disclosure, during the night, and on Valentine's Day, that she no longer wished to be in a relationship with him. Because his season was kicking off, contracts and calendars were being finalised, tickets were being finalised, she had to give him her commitment. More than that: *It was Valentine's Day*. What a day for the practical reality of his life, and her life, and the logistical incompatibility of their lives to finally surface.

From March onwards, Reeva suddenly realised, Oscar would be spending months broad. After competing in Manchester in May, Oscar would remain at his Italian home base to complete the European Season. That meant she'd be without her boo for as many as six months at a time. But Reeva had been there before with Lahoud. No! She had learnt her lesson. Not again. *I can't go through that again*. She discloses her unhappiness and her loneliness, in this regard, on Facebook. And to console Oscar, she may have told him about how it was with Warren. But what about his plans for them to move in together? She'd also moved in with Warren, and lived in his empty house. She'd eventually bought a parrot to help her face the hours and empty rooms without him [see *Reeva in her own Words*]. No, Oscar I just can't go through that again.

Late at night, remembering she had met her ex-boyfriend just hours earlier (just 36 hours earlier,

http://www.express.co.uk/news/world/463838/Reeva-Steenkamp-hap-planned-go-home-night-she-was-shot

and Oscar had called *twice* during that meeting), Oscar may have felt himself unravelling. His career about to fire him off again, like Icarous. Never had his brand shined so bright. But his journey to the sun would be cold, his sole companion the Withering Wind of Loneliness. To be so cruelly rejected then, on Valentine's Day...

And that was the Invalidation of the *private* persona. His unprotected self, the primary part of him he revealed to no one, but had unconcealed to Reeva, was suffering. A raw, existential anguish. His entire overarching sense of self, the inner man and the outer man, were cauterised by the intrusion of real life. On Valentine's Day we ask ourselves:

Who loves me? Does anybody love me?

For all his heroism, the state of things, the state of his world, would remain brutal. This was life's answer to Oscar. This was the double blow on Valentine's Day. I won't be part of your career. *And* I won't be part of your life either. I love you, Oscar, but I can't do it again.

The world was on fire and no one could save me but you
It's strange what desire will make foolish people do
I'd never dreamed that I'd meet somebody like you
I'd never dreamed that I'd lose somebody like you

No I don't want to fall in love (this girl is only gonna break your heart)
No I don't want to fall in love (this girl is only gonna break your heart)
With you
With you (this girl is only gonna break your heart)

What a wicked game you played to make me feel this way
what a wicked thing to do to let me dream of you
what a wicked thing to say you never felt this way
what a wicked thing to do to make me dream of you

Realtors say it's all about location, location, location. Murder is about motive, but motive in a case where there is no confession, no admission of wrongdoing and only circumstantial evidence means you end up with hundreds if not thousands of clues. Pieces to a puzzle. Do you have all of them? Do all the piece belong. Do they fit or, in our efforts to form a narrative, are we forcing a fit when there isn't one. It gets trickier the closer you are to the narrative. You can be too close so you drown in the minutiae. Or too far that you can't see an essential clue. If professional safe distance is mastered somehow, and all the clues have been assembled, the investigator must then turn to the one thing that sharpens and crystallises the half formed puzzle taking shape. And that's Context. Part of context, in our reframing, our interrogation of Oscar's narrative, is Intent. Intent in turn is Motive's ugly cousin.

Let's turn back, very briefly, look for the real context, and examine the athlete's real intentions. What is it we want answered? What context are we looking to clarify? Just this:

What exactly was happening in Oscar's life? What was happening in his career? And what were his intentions towards Reeva? We know they were elaborate. He thought they would move in together. He thought they would travel around the world together (within weeks of the incident). He thought she'd be part of his career, and wanted to make her part of his life. But how can we be certain about the extent of Oscar's intentions (besides via his own account)? One man who has provided absolutely key contextual insights into Oscar life's is his agent. In fact, there is no better man to bear witness to this. Besides Reeva, Peet Van Zyl is as close to the horse's mouth as we are ever going to get. He's the man closest to Oscar's inner circle. He's right there, the man with the contracts, the schemes, the timetables. He's got bags of firsthand knowledge. Not only about Oscar, but also Reeva and the whole brand ambassadorial spiel* (which he was facilitating in the background). So let's interrogate him.

Van Zyl knew exactly what forces were circling around the couple, and specifically congregating in his client, which is why when Nel broached the subject Oscar's representative could hardly speak.

The prologue to this vital line of questioning (Nel to Van Zyl) was Nel catching out Van Zyl on his many (apparent) failures. Firstly to manage and mentor his client on reckless driving and then Oscar's gun love. Van Zyl said it wasn't his job to know everything about his client (actually, as Wicksell tells us, a good agent is like a father figure, so it was his job). But if failed to fluster Van Zyl on the topic of cars and guns, Nel was effective at riling Oscar's agent on an issue of emotion. How had he handled Oscar's roommate's evacuation? In fact, at one point the agent said – when accused of cheating, unfairness, he often got more angry than Oscar did. The reader should also be aware that Van Zyl, at the time of Oscar's boating accident, blamed the fact that his client was on the river late at night. We know that Oscar said in court that he crashed the boat because he had been blinded by the setting sun. Who is lying?

As soon as Nel had Van Zyl sufficiently flustered, he went for the jugular.

Nel: "Did you discuss the incident with Mr Pistorius?"

Van Zyl: [Voice trembling] "Did I ...eh...discuss the incident (out of breath)..."

Van Zyl is almost stuttering. He splutters something about "working on planning these trips together" and giving Oscar his condolences.

Nel: "Apart from sending him your condolences. The question is fairly simple. Did you discuss the incident since the 14 February?"

Van Zyl: [Voice still trembling] "No my lady I have not discussed the specifics of the incidents with Mr Pistorius at all."

Nel: "Not once?"

Van Zyl: "Not once. Mr Pistorius never discussed what happened. I did not ask him. And that I can state...... (voice trails off)"

Nel then let's Van Zyl off the hook and takes a different tack.

Nel: "Mr Pistorius' love for guns – do you know about that?"

Van Zyl says he was aware of Oscar carrying a gun for the first time in November 2012. The Sokolove article (mentioning Van Zyl) was in fact published at the beginning of 2012, January 18 to be exact. But Van Zyl maintains he was unaware of Oscar's gun ownership and speeding habits.

Now let's get to the key question. And it relates to Motive. Why was Van Zyl so nervous when Nel peppered him on the night of the incident. Had Oscar and Van Zyl discussed it?

Before we look at Van Zyl's answers, has he proved a believable witness thus far?

In his brief time on the stand on 1 July, Nel said to Van Zyl: Why don't you answer the question? Is it so difficult to say something negative about Oscar?

Also, consider the context again. On February 13, sometime after 7pm, Van Zyl is hard at work making arrangements to get his client (and Reeva) on a plane to Manchester. That event is in May.

A week earlier both athlete and agent had discussed Reeva's role in Oscar career, and both had phoned her on the 7th, following extensive planning. Now Van Zyl was executing those plans and arrangements Oscar and he had thrashed out.

But what do we know?

1. We know Oscar and Peet van Zyl planned a schedule on 7 February, and invited Reeva to be part of it. Pertinently, they had invited Reeva to participate in Oscar's CAREER. This meant she would be part of his 'team', and contractual arrangements would include her. Furthermore, there was more than one contract in play on the 13th of February, and Oscar himself had shared his intent. Ironically when Gerrie Nel noted the reasons why Oscar wanted Reeva to travel with him – to see him and his world, Oscar was seen chuckling.

2. But was Reeva ready to give up her career? We know on 13 February Reeva met with her publicist at Capacity Relations, and we know both Sarit Tomlinson (the CEO) and Simphiwe Majola didn't think Oscar's brand was good for hers.

3. We also know that after previously suggesting she would cook dinner for Oscar on Thursday, Valentine's Day, she subsequently suggested he spend time with his family. Oscar, in contrast, repeatedly asked her to come over, and spend the night, but Reeva seemed to intuit that this would inevitably lead to a confrontation.

   a) "What happened at Capacity Relations?"

   b) "Have you decided, are you coming with me to Brazil? What about Manchester? What about Italy?"

   c) Reeva would have asked, possibly, what this would have involved and Oscar would have said several weeks, even months abroad. Whether together or not, the implications would be either protracted periods apart, or the death knell to her career (certainly an interruption or rerouting of her career. Both these scenarios would have been untenable for her. Firstly because she was highly invested in her own career, and had her own contracts and obligations to fulfil. Secondly because she had endured long periods of separation with Warren Lahoud.

d) Reeva also uncharacteristically cancelled an engagement with a major sponsor, Nimue, at short notice, to do damage control with Oscar, who we already know 'needed consoling'

4. From Oscar's side the stakes were staggeringly high. For the first time in his career he faced a real threat (on equal footing, so to speak) from Brazil's Oliveira. (The Oliveira threat hasn't been an empty one either, in 2013 he set world records over the 100m and 200m distances. If Oliveira eclipsed him, Oscar risked losing his monopoly on the moniker: 'fastest man on no legs'. Arguably, it had already happened in London, 2012.

5. The walls were also moving in terms of the broad scientific criticism around the fairness of Oscar's singular participation (as a disabled athlete) with able-bodied athletes. Tucker was part of this assault, so were authoritative journalists in Spain, England (the BBC) and the USA. Big names such as Michael Johnson were also against his participation. In other words, the clock was ticking both in terms of Oscar's dominance of the Paralympian scene and also his claim as being 'uniquely' talented.

6. And we also know that based on Whatsapp and other social media messages, the bubble of lovey dovey messages popped on February 13. Instead of excitement about romantic overseas adventures together, there were suggestions, from Reeva to Oscar that he 'spend time with his family', and she used the word 'console'. Remember, Oscar is trying to get her business class tickets, include her in his business contracts. But Reeva isn't interested. She's interested in Oscar – the person – not his career.

7. The athletics season for Oscar typically starts in February. Reeva would have been made aware that if she didn't accompany Oscar overseas, they would be apart for many – perhaps as many as six – months at a time. Oscar didn't want to go overseas on his own, and appeared desperate for a long term companion, and otherwise, appeared generally lonely. And needing company. If Reeva joined Oscar she would have to sacrifice her career, or at the very least, damage it, and at a time when everything was coming together for her.

8. Huge amounts of money were at stake. Van Zyl said Oscar's net worth had been leveraged by around six fold. But if his brand was teetering in the dizzy heights of celebrity, it was also twisting dangerously in the strong headwinds of public – and scientific – scrutiny. His entire narrative was at real risk of implosion. His outburst against Oliveira had shown that.

There's your context.

Now let's sketch a scenario with this almost-complete picture of circumstantial evidence.

It is unlikely then, given the above information, that Reeva planned to stay the night. She would have tried to console Oscar, but he would have felt rejected on two levels. Firstly, his career ambitions (for her, and with her) had been scuppered. This betrayal was compounded, possibly, by an admission that the relationship wasn't going to work. Not if he was overseas for half the year. A double blow like that on the day before Valentine's Day would have been devastating to Oscar. It would mean travelling to all these far flung destinations alone, and single, and having to face a barrage of cynical reporters everywhere he went. Would he, could he, stay on top of Oliveira? Was it all slipping away just as it seemed to be coming together so perfectly? Why, he would have cried, don't you just come with me? Do you know who I am? How much I am worth.

Reeva, realising he couldn't be consoled, would have wanted to go home, but this would have upset him even more. Don't go. But when she stayed, the confrontation simply went on. He would have pestered her and tried to convince her. After all, playing in the back of his mind, his agent was arranging their tickets that very night. Please, please, would she, could she reconsider. But the more he went on the more she felt trapped. And then, anyone of a thousand triggers could have set of the tinderbox that had been rigged. Her meeting with Warren Lahoud several hours earlier, had he something to do with her change of heart, her change of mind? No. And what about his girlfriends?

Having argued for most of the night, Reeva had sms'd her best friend to say it was too late, she wouldn't be returning home. She then settled down to a late supper.

What happened after that?

Perhaps another argument flared up. A midnight message? Perhaps Oscar couldn't sleep. When Reeva went to the toilet, Oscar may have suspected that she might use her phone to call for help. Call the police. Perhaps that what she said when he stormed to the door (out of bed, on his stumps).

What are you doing? I knew I couldn't trust you!

By now Reeva would have been hysterical. She would have locked the door, and since she had her phone, tried to bargain with him. And in this situation, Oscar would have felt defeated. Out of control. If she called the police, called anyone, and word of this 'abusive' argument got out, all his ambitions, all his events, would be wrecked before he had set foot on the first plane. He had to control that narrative. He had to prevent Reeva from using her phone, or leaving the house. His life was at stake. His millions, about to go up in smoke. Even if she didn't call, she couldn't be allowed to leave. No one could know what happened here.

If he killed her, he could make up his own story. The media, the police, the neighbours, all would listen to his story.

The first bullet was fired at the sound. He stabilised himself against the wall, saw the light of her phone coming from under the door. He could hear her screaming inside, even though the second bullet missed. He needed to wait so his ears could clear, to hear where she was. Then he fired the third shot. By now he knew exactly where she was. And then he fired the fourth, and her screams died away. Somewhere during this commotion he went to the balcony and also shouted for help. He was already trying to protect his brand, which, in time, with the best legal team money could buy, he'd resurrect.

Is that what happened?

* http://dictionary.reference.com/browse/spiel
**Note: 'Startled' is the same word used by the Defence's expert witness, Professor Derman (Day 37). Both Derman and Nel use this word to reference triggers that set off Oscar's amgydala hijacking (or flooding).

Conclusion

"Life has become immeasurably better since I have been forced to stop taking it seriously," – Hunter S. Thompson [Quoted by Lance on Lance Armstrong's twitter profile]

When one considers the actual content of Oscar's 'version', everything that happens to Reeva (she's trapped, terrified, screaming) also happens to Oscar. Furthermore, what he must do is neither see nor hear Reeva, and then all we are left with is a door. And that's basically what the whole trial hinges on. Four shots through a closed door. There is no getting around that.

Consider though, in Oscar's version he snuffs Reeva ought visually. He makes it so dark he can't see her. He also snuffs her out audibly. He reduces who she is, that vital life to nothing more than an anonymous noise. And then robs her of a voice, after her death, by saying her screams were his. In the same way her existence, her life was stolen from her in reality (she was shot dead), Oscar's version also snuffs her out. We don't see her, hear her, we don't know where she is, what's she's doing, how she's feeling, what's she's saying. In contrast we know all these things about Oscar. Why?

Because it's all about Oscar.

Oscar expects a lot. He expects us to accept that four shots through a closed, locked door were accidental. He also expects us to accept that Reeva didn't scream, and he never saw her – at all – in the minute/s it took him to move from one end of the bedroom to the bathroom. He's hypervigilant, but didn't see her, hear her *or make any attempt* to do either. Why not?

In his athletics career he has also expected a lot from us. He expects us to accept that he is unique (he's not), that his legs give him no advantage (they give him enormous advantages), and that it's fair for him to compete against able-bodied runners (it isn't). He expects to be able to compete at not just one Olympics, but two. In the same way he asks us to accept four bullets through a closed door, and not a single scream, he also asks too much of us as a disabled athlete.

Disabled athlete. Able-bodied athlete. Disabled means immobilised. It means Stop. Hinder. Halt. Put out of action. Oscar did all these things to Reeva. But he expects us to accept his excuses and explanations, so he can be mobilised, so he can get back into action. It's not going to happen.

Remember Oscar's first agent? Not Peet van Zyl, the guy who broke the 24 minute mile 24 times. In fact I did an article on Ray Wicksell for Fitness Magazine (His Edition, the July-August 2014 issue) under the title, *Breaking Barriers*. The question this narrative has sought to interrogate is basically this:

Should Oscar's attempt to compete against able-bodied athletes be allowed? Is it fair? Is it a *valid narrative* in the first place, and from a scientific and an ethical stand-point, should we support (or have supported) Oscar in these efforts? At breaking barriers. At breaking through?

RESURRECTION echoes the same arguments as Tucker, Johnson, Weyand, McEvoy, Sokolove and Wicksell. Remember what Wicksell said at the outset?

"What I wanted him to do for many years, even when he was with Peet [Oscar's agent, and Wicksell's successor], and I haven't spoken to many people about this, only my wife and Oscar, I wanted him to go around the world. Because he's well known now. And I wanted him to go to Mexico, I wanted him to go to Argentina, I wanted him to go to Cuba, I wanted him to go to the United States. Go to Africa. And tell the Oscar Story. How to become a champion in life. You know, not only in work, but in life. And that's what I wanted him to do. And then I wanted him to come out with a book; he came out with his book. But then I wanted him to go into these talks. I mean, he would have been such a wonderful speaker, on stage. Because it comes natural for him. That's what I always wanted him to do."

Then Wicksell pauses. "At one stage," he says, "I told Carte Blanche, 'You know, he will bounce back.' I thought that, if he gets acquitted he might still be able to run the Olympics again. Because, you know, if he's innocent, people forget and forgive very, very quick. If someone is innocent. So I said 'Yes, he'll be back. He's got it in his blood.'"

The addendum to this statement hinges on one tiny little word: "If." If Oscar has been honest. If Oscar has been innocent. And by the same token, if his agent (Van Zyl), who has been perpetuating the same narrative, has been honest in his defence, and support and endorsement of the disabled money-spinner. Has he? Have they? Then, to quote McEvoy:

Why, then, the doubters?

Because any (and hopefully every) reasonable thinking person ought to be doubtful. Wicksell says Oscar should never have gone the able-bodied route. He would still have been a champion. He would still have been successful and highly regarded and wealthy. The attempt to compete against able-bodied athletes, by a disabled athlete, using advanced materials that don't flex, get injured or fatigued creates a fiasco. A circus, as we've seen.

My personal view is Reeva, though she had strong feelings, though she was committed and invested, she was also doubtful. If you have seen Oscar without his legs, you've seen that clearly, he's not an athlete. Capacity Relations were doubtful. And as it turned out, Reeva's doubt, in tragic retrospect, was entirely justified. But what about the rest of us? Are we able to see things for what they are?

Virginia Woolf once wrote: "To look life in the face, always, to look life in the face, and to know it for what it is...at last, to love it for what it is, and then, to put it away..." Can we do this for Oscar? Can we do this for ourselves? Because without total honesty, there's going to be constant trauma, without honesty there's never *Resurrection*.

http://www.huffingtonpost.com/2014/05/22/norm-macdonald-oscar-pistorius-conan-video_n_5374895.html

Author's Note:

The next, the fourth eBook in this series is ~~Restitutio~~ *Revelations*. In it we'll probe 14 unanswered questions. We'll get the views from Dr Ross Tucker. We'll look at how the IAAF ought to handle the plight of disabled athletes fairly – and honestly – going forward. And ~~we'll begin to turn this whole narrative around, to pursue how we can turn a negative into a positive. How can we learn from our mistakes? Why are we so afraid of being wrong? What is the nature of transcendence (away from the Oscar Trial), in our personal lives. In our world~~ we'll interrogate what ACTUALLY happened on the 13/14th of February.

Kathryn Schulz, author of Being Wrong, Adventures in the margin of error, says that *looking for counterevidence – as I have – often requires time, energy, learning, liberty, and sufficient social capital –* that's you *– to weather the suspicion and derision of defenders of the status quo.*

Eventually, after revevlations, we must find a way to turn this exhausting, negative narrative into something affirming. I think Reeva would like that. I like the idea of a bursary, in her name, which goes to a female student interested in studying law. Perhaps, if we – her supporters – can come together collectively, we can put something together. Perhaps we can achieve some sort of *restitutio ad integrum*.

Perhaps Reeva's family – Barry, or June, or Kim – can sell a story to an international publication, an exclusive, and use the proceeds to set up this special fund for Reeva. Perhaps we the public can rally together as well. It would be an annual bursary at Reeva's alma mater, the Nelson Mandela Metropolitan University (NMMU).

Reeva, one day, having sought her fortune and having seen the world, planned to return home to Port Elizabeth or Cape Town. Having lived a full life, and then some, she would have felt ready for a more serious phase. Without the tiara, practising law.

I think it would be a fitting legacy to her story, her once-rising star, if every year we – the South African public, and the communities beyond, the enormous collective of social capital that cares about this case – wouldn't it be great if we gave one deserving young woman a chance, a real start, at bringing to life the very journey that was stolen from Reeva. That realisation would be a small gesture from us. Our gift, on behalf of a beautiful woman with a big heart.

We could give her a last chance, for one last, warm, knowing smile. It would give Reeva's story, and the life that was stolen from her, a real chance at *Resurrection*.

Author's Update [11 November 2014]

I write this missive to you on the other side of time. 22 months ago Reeve Steenkamp posted this message to Instagram:

My new apartment will have one of these guys in it ...
http://instagram.com/p/UrK8zewPbw/

But there is no new apartment for her or 'one of those guys'. Now Reeva is dead, and her boyfriend is in jail. But not for her murder. For killing her *accidentally*.

22 months ago Reeva hadn't even met Oscar.

5 months ago, when we started this journey to *Resurrection*, we neither knew the verdict or the sentence. Now we have both, with an appeal slated for December 6.

We're also told Oscar's defence will oppose the appeal, this despite claims that Oscar is broken (and a 'broken man').

We've also learned* that Oscar's neighbour in Pretoria's Kgosi Mampuru Prison right now is none other than the notorious Radovan Krejčíř:

Two weeks ago, City Press reported that Pistorius was broke after having racked up a R17.5 million legal bill, about R10 million of which is still unpaid.

Pistorius has been moved to the B section of the prison near the hospital wing, where he has his own private cell. Among his neighbours is Czech fugitive Radovan Krejčíř, whom City Press understands has his own television in his cell that is hooked up to DStv.

Krejčíř also celebrated his birthday in prison this week and he shared his birthday cake, which was delivered to the prison, with the other prisoners in the wing, including Pistorius…

On 22 November, it will be Oscar's turn. Oscar will celebrate his 28th birthday in jail. Will he return the favour, and share birthday cake with Krejčíř? And if he does, what else will they share?

Prison authorities meanwhile have been at pains to stress that a bath constructed for Oscar (and for his sole use) is not being constructed for Oscar, but has been 'under construction for some time'…

And just how dapper is the 'Blade Runner' in his new orange uniform?

…Pistorius, who does not mingle with other prisoners, even at meal times, has become extremely depressed in jail.

His fellow inmates, sources say, have even been encouraging him to see the prison counsellor.

They have told him "he would not be regarded as a sissie" if he asked for help. "He has even cried on occasion," said the source. "He really is battling with prison."

Sources say that <u>Pistorius is apparently frustrated by the fact that everyone around him is so negative.</u> "Other inmates and wardens feel sorry for him or ashamed of his fall from grace and keep burdening him with their feelings," the source said.

<u>"He is so tired of everybody wanting something from him and just wants to think positively</u> and believe in God that his ordeal will soon be over."

Soon…may be ~~10~~ 9 months time. Will Oscar's resurrection begin then, in earnest? Will the world embrace his like a prodigal son? Will his family's unwavering support…begin to waver?

City Press was also told that Afrikaans-speaking inmates were looking out for him.

"They have his back, he won't get into any trouble as he is being protected," he said.

Not likely. Oscar's *Resurrection* is far from over…

* *http://www.citypress.co.za/news/oscar-pistorius-gets-private-bath/*

About the Author

<u>Nick van der Leek</u> is a South African photojournalist and storyteller with an unconventional background. Instead of journalism he studied law, economics and brand management. His writing career started online, as a blogger in South Korea and a citizen journalist for Seoul-based Ohmynews International. After cutting his teeth in Rosebank, Johannesburg at AVUSA (now Times Media), he became a full-time writer and photographer, and today he is one of South Africa's most diverse freelancers. Although he has a penchant for research and analysis his passion is creating, analysing and leveraging narratives. He is currently working on the final book in his BLOODLINE series, a post-apocalyptic, dystopian, sci fi epic set in Scotland and outer space.

Follow him on twitter: <u>@HiRezLife</u>

www.ingramcontent.com/pod-product-compliance
Lightning Source LLC
Chambersburg PA
CBHW071755200526
45167CB00018B/1840